Christian Reunion

It Is Required of Stewards

John M. McBain
It Is Required
of Stewards

Broadman Press
Nashville, Tennessee

1697

Contents

It Is Required of Stewards

1.
Stewardship Is Theological— Man's Place in God's World

I fear that sometimes we Christians today are a little prone to misuse this perfectly good word "stewardship." Stewardship is not synonymous with "money-raising." Stewardship is not a plan for raising funds. Stewardship is not tithing. Tithing is a part of stewardship. It is involved in the subject of stewardship, but stewardship is much broader than this. Now we commonly broaden it by saying that stewardship includes time and talents as well as our treasures. This is true. But I am still of the conviction that stewardship is even deeper than this.

I asked a very good friend of mine, Dr. W. H. Allison, to tell me what he considered the real significance of tithing. He answered: "My emphasis on stewardship all the way along has been theological. I believe, from the very first years that I got acquainted with the doctrine, that stewardship is just as much a part of the theology of the Word of God as the plan of redemption, the second coming of Christ, or the security of the believer. Therefore, my methods have been to teach the basic principles of Bible stewardship and thus give a foundation for tithing or more. When we seek to get our people to tithe on the basis of the missionary need of today we are starting at the wrong end. We are attempting to pick the fruit before the vine has matured. Tithing should be the fruits or the results of basic theological teaching that pertains to total stewardship as undergirding everything the believer is and does. The fact is, total stewardship is the term that describes the believer's commission from God to be in God's program at all. The believer is made a child by salvation through the blood of Christ. He is made an obedient child and thus will be rewarded on the basis of his good stewardship. All individuals, however, whether they are saved or lost, are stewards. This is pointed out in Genesis 1:28 when God commissioned the first couple as stewards.

"Proportionate giving probably is a better term and ought to be used to describe basic giving for believers. The word 'tithe' has a tendency to narrow one's giving to just 10 percent. New Testament giving may be 90 percent given and 10 percent retained as a working capital." He gives a quotation from Dr. Edward B. Willingham, a Baptist preacher in the American Baptist Convention who said, "those who tithe know that the principle is not one of legalism but that it is a token of complete dedication of life and property to the will and purpose of God. Tithing is a minimum below which love dares not stoop."

Concerning tithing, Dr. Allison gives these three statements: "In the Old Testament there were apparently three regular tithes. (1) the first tithe went to the tribe of Levi. This was for the support of the Levites, for the support of the priesthood. (2) The second tithe went for tabernacle services, for worship and feast periods. These tithes were already paid for when the people came together. (3) The third tithe apparently was followed every third year. The first two tithes were taken to the tabernacle and to the priesthood. The third tithe was kept at home and was used to help the stranger, the orphan, the widow, and so forth.

"Besides these, there were voluntary offerings every year. No Jew would be considered in right relationship to his God who did less. This again is theological. They were just as basic in their theology as were the sacrifices for sin covering, and so forth." These statements of Dr. Allison's serve as background and introduction, not for tithing but for basic stewardship.

The Earth Is the Lord's

Paul says in 2 Corinthians 5:19: "God was in Christ reconciling the world unto himself." What did Paul mean by "world" in that text? We are familiar with the world in John 3:16, the exact same word, same form in the Greek in John 3:16 as in 2 Corinthians 5:19. When we look at John 3:16, we preach loud and long that God loved the whole world, all people. Well, that's good preaching. I believe it. But is this all that he meant when he said "the world." The world includes not only people. The word that is used is "cosmos." This includes the first definition, for it has to do with the material world. It was used sometimes in the New Testament to refer to the whole human race and mankind. But its *first* definition in my lexicon is for the material world.

Now, with stewardship as the concept, I suggest to you that Jesus was not only redeeming people. God's whole world is lost. Because it seems as though man, who was given responsibility over the care of the world, went off and took the world with him. And God wants to reconcile the world of things, also. The Bible says that the silver and the gold are the Lord's. But the silver and the gold are not in God's treasury. They are in the hands of men. The psalmist says "the cattle upon the thousand hills" are the Lord's. Does the cattleman who sells them at the market realize this? Or is he selling his own cattle? This is basic stewardship. I think you can see that Dr. Allison was right when he said, "stewardship is basically theological." Stewardship is theological because it is involved in our concept of God and in our concept of man and their relationship one to another. God, who is God? How big is your God? Assuming that we are all conservative theologians, I could assume that we all believe in the immediate creation of our world by the hand of God.

There are some people who don't believe this. I think they have undercut the real basis of stewardship as well as departing from our Bible concept of creation. What is the basis of God's ownership of our world? He made it. So we go back to Genesis and we find the creation of our world. This is the starting point of stewardship.

In Genesis 1:28–30 we read: "God blessed them and God said unto them, Be fruitful, and multiply, and replenish the earth, and subdue it: and have dominion over the fish of the sea, and over the fowl of the air, and over every living thing that moveth upon the earth. And God said, Behold, I have given you every herb bearing seed, which is upon the face of all the earth, and every tree, in the which is the fruit of a tree yielding seed; to you it shall be for meat. And to every beast of the earth, and to every fowl of the air, and to everything that creepeth upon the earth, wherein there is life, I have given every green herb for meat: and it was so." In the second chapter of Genesis (2:15), we read "And the Lord God took the man, and put him into the Garden of Eden to dress it and to keep it." This is stewardship. Man was to take care of God's garden.

Let me digress to define a term. Our word "steward," as it is found in the New Testament, is a translation of the Greek word from which our English word "economy" comes. The lexicon says that this word which is the root of our word economy was a word that was used in relationship to household management. For example, when a man had a servant or a slave who was of perhaps unusual ability, he might be given the responsibility of the administration of affairs of the household. Archaeologists have discovered that this word "economy" has been found in such common things as shopping lists. "Economy" was concerned with the operation of the household, the buying of food, the handling of the money to pay for the operation of the household. The slave who was made responsible for this—everything from the shopping to the book-keeping—was the steward. He was the man responsible for the economics of the house. This is the background of our Christian word "steward." In the stewardship parables, as we call them, from the lips of our Lord there are parables dealing with the actual economics of the collection of debts and so forth that was in the hands of a servant? He was a steward. This ought to help give us a picture of what a steward is. We should also take note of the fact that in the Synoptic Gospels, we are told, one verse in every six has to do with man's stewardship or relationship to material things. I think we've brought some discredit on stewardship because we've never preached on it except when we were either low on the church treasury or it was time to raise a budget. Stewardship has become a fund-raising concept, which is absolutely unbiblical.

What is man? God or gardener? This is theological. What is man? God or gardener? Our concept of God and our concept of man have to come to play against each other at this point. In Genesis 2:15 we find that God is God, the God who created the heavens and the earth, the one that placed man in the garden and told him to prune the bushes and pluck the fruit. But it was God's garden.

The prophets, such as Jonah, when asked who he was, where he came from, where he was going, and what was his religion, said, "My God is the God that created the heavens and the earth." And those on the ship decided that Jonah must be sacrificed to the gods because he apparently worshiped the biggest God and the storm would be calm if Jonah's problem could be settled. Well, isn't that the biggest God in the world, the one that created the world? When the apostle Paul got to Athens and was trying to confront the intellectuals with the simple gospel, he confronted them on the basis of their ignorance. He said: "He whom you ignorantly worship, I have come to declare unto you," and Paul identified his God as the God who created the heavens and the earth. This is our Christian God. Some of the casualness with which modern Christianity uses God and the church and the Bible is as if passing through some sort of a religious cafeteria where you take what you want, leave the rest, and hope that the bill isn't too high. We could overcome a lot of this casualness in religion if we could once again convince people that they are worshiping the God who created the heavens and the earth. But the theology of the modern Christian who sits in the sanctuary every Sunday morning has been watered down by his having been exposed to a common acceptance of evolution. God isn't very big anymore. Our theology has to come back into play here. It relates to our worship, it relates to our discipleship, and it relates to our stewardship.

In the third chapter of Genesis we find that sin came into the world. At the basis of the doctrine of original sin actually is the violation of the law of stewardship. Man was not supposed to be owner of the garden. The owner has complete right and freedom of reservation. The owner has the right to make reservations. In the business world when reservations are made in contracts, the violation of the reservation means the canceling of the contract. Here is a man and a woman who were placed in the garden and given the task of being gardeners. But the devil put the temptations before them. "Now the serpent was more subtil than any beast of the field which the Lord God had made. And he said unto the woman, Yea, hath God said, ye shall not eat of every tree of the garden?" (Gen. 3:1). You know that today the devil is still questioning whether God ever said it or not.

And the woman said unto the serpent, "We may eat of the fruit of the trees of the garden." We may. This is permission. She is recognizing the authority of God the owner. She said: "We may eat of the fruit of the trees of the garden: but of the fruit of the tree which is in the midst of the garden, God hath said, Ye shall not eat of it, neither shall ye touch it, lest ye die." And the serpent said unto the woman, "Ye shall not surely die." Again he questions the authority of God. "For God doth know that in the day you eat thereof, then your eyes shall be opened, and ye shall be as gods knowing good and evil. And when the woman saw that the tree was good for food, and that it was pleasant to the eyes, and a tree to be desired to make one wise, she took of the fruit thereof, and did eat, and gave also unto her husband with her; and he did eat." I believe the third temptation was the one that got the woman. She could "be as a god" and she would rather be a goddess than a gardener's wife. Actually the original sin was a matter of steward-ship, because the man and woman were supposed to take care of the garden according to the instructions and under the authority of the owner, which was God.

Now if you will take this thought and follow it all the way through the Bible, you will see that this relationship of stewardship still prevails in the New Testament. This is man's place—he is to take care of God's world. Consequently, when I look at sin in the sense I've just presented it to you and then I look at 2 Corinthians 5:19 and see that God was in Christ reconciling the world unto himself, I see that actually God lost the whole garden. I would like to point out that God was not evicting a poor tenant. He was firing a dishonest gardener! This is the way God still deals with people if they do not properly handle that which is his, he reserves the right to take it away from them. But man must see himself as a steward, as a manager of somebody else's affairs, always subject to report to the owner, to the Lord, to God. I read for example Romans 14:12, "Every one of us shall give an account of himself to God." I refer to this as a stewardship report. "Everyone of us shall give an account of himself to God." Our own selves, our lives, our bodies are themselves involved in stewardship.

The Fulness Thereof

Remember Psalm 24:1 where the psalmist says, "The earth is the Lord's, and the fulness thereof; the world and they that dwell therein." I take this verse to substantiate what I suggested to you about the world. He makes a distinction between the earth and the world. The earth and the fulness thereof, these are the Lord's. That's the good earth, the ground where you plant the seeds. I remember a professor in seminary used to quote that verse, "the earth is the Lord's and the 'fruitfulness' thereof." I think that is a good valid interpretation. The earth and the fruitfulness thereof. God owns the field, and God owns the orange tree, and he owns the oranges. The earth is the Lord's, he created it, and I believe he owns that orchard out there that one of my deacons operates by a title of love. And he is going to give an account to God for what he does with the fruit on every one of those trees as much as Adam did. Because the usefulness of that fruit is God's business, it is God's fruit. There is a stewardship involved in which we work together.

In Psalm 50:9–12 the psalmist points out the ownership of God when he says, "I will take no bullock out of thy house nor he goats out of thy folds. For every beast of the forest is mine and the cattle upon a thousand hills. I know all the fowls of the mountains and the wild beast of the fields are mine." (Now get the sarcasm of this, if you will allow such a reference to God.) "If I were hungry, I would not tell thee: for the world is mine, and the fulness thereof." The *fruitfulness* thereof.

When we present the stewardship "challenge" on the basis of the needs of the church and the needs of the missionaries, I have a problem with this passage. Paul said, (Acts 17:25) that it was not that God had need of anything. God isn't poor. The silver and the gold and the cattle upon the thousand hills are his. Then why is it we are called upon to put our pennies and our nickels and our dimes into the offering plate on Sunday? Why do we have this emphasis on fund raising in our churches? God is not poor. Why does man then have to subsidize God's program? Because God doesn't have any wheat fields or orchards except the ones that are tended by men. They are God's, it is true. And God's program for the redemption of the world involves that orchard out there every bit as much as it involves the young man that walks down the aisle on Sunday morning and says, "I feel called to be a missionary." One man is recognizing the stewardship of his life in terms of talents, another man is recognizing the stewardship of his life in terms of possession. But both of these are conditioned on the fact that we ourselves and all of this world are God's. We are stewards, that's all. When I am called upon to prune the saints and pluck the fruits of the church, I'm just as much a husbandman of God, as Paul phrased it, as the man that picks the oranges and the grapefruit from God's orchard. It's just a question of which field you are working in. The church is God's. Christ said, "I will build my church." It's his. But he doesn't own the church any more than he owns the orchards, nor vice versa. Wherever your life or mine is to be invested, you must always acknowledge the authority of God as the creator of heaven and earth.

Suppose that we were to take the narrow concept that many take on this matter of reconciliation of the world to God and think of it in terms of preaching of sermons and the winning of converts in the sense of repentance and faith. This calls for missionaries. This calls for witnesses. This calls for preachers. How are you going to carry on a program like this? God's program of world redemption, you can call it world missions if you like, has been waiting for the redemption of the oil wells and the orchards and the wheat fields and the factories that are in the hands of unregenerated men. The tragedy is that we preachers have made the error of thinking and leading a man to think that he can be saved without any effect on his material possessions or his employment or his condition of servitude. Redemption includes the total life. God is not only concerned about the soul of the individual. If he were, salvation would be nothing but a fire escape from hell. It's more than this if I understand my Bible. And the man that has a good understanding of genuine redemption in terms of his soul will realize that until the world of life is surrendered, he is not really a Christian. And this is stewardship. It begins with the redemption of man with the understanding that not only this spiritual entity that we call "soul" is involved, but man's total life which involves all of his human contacts and all of his human involvements in the affairs of the world must be redeemed. We need to redeem farms in order to support missions. That's God's purpose out there, that they might be saved. But there is another reason for this. I believe that our relationship to material things is involved in our covenant relationship with God as Christians.

Let's go back to the Old Testament, to Deuteronomy the eighth chapter. Moses warned the Israelites concerning the perils of prosperity. In verses 9–14 He said: "Beware that thou forget not the Lord thy God, in not keeping his commandments, and his judgments, and his statutes, which I command thee this day." Why were they in danger of forgetting it? In the preceding verses he said, "A land wherein thou shalt eat bread without scarceness, thou shalt not lack anything in it; a land whose stones are iron, and out of whose hills thou mayest dig brass. When thou hast eaten and art full, then thou shalt bless the Lord thy God for the good land which he hath given thee." Beware that thou shalt forget not thy God. This is stewardship. "Lest when thou hast eaten and art full, and hast built goodly houses, and dwelt therein; and when thy herds and thy flocks multiply, and thy silver and thy gold is multiplied, and all that thou hast is multiplied; Then thine heart be lifted up, and thou forget the Lord thy God, which brought thee forth out of the land of Egypt from the house of bondage." Don't forget, you are just a servant, a steward. "And thou say in thine heart, My power and the might of mine hand hath gotten me this wealth." "But thou shalt remember the Lord thy God: for it is he that giveth thee power to get wealth that he may establish his covenant which he sware unto thy fathers, as it is this day" (vv. 17–18). The Revised Standard Version translates this "that he may confirm his covenant." Your material prosperity as God's people is merely a confirmation of God's covenant. After all, had he not promised Abraham and his seed this land flowing of milk and honey? And the fact that you now have it is only the confirmation and the establishment of the carrying out of God's covenant. But in it they were not to forget God.

I believe this same thing pertains in the day of Abraham, the day of Jacob, when each of them practiced tithing. This was simply the public testimony of their acknowledgement of their stewardship relationship to God. Man must see his place. Stewardship is theological.

The World and They That Dwell Therein

In the New Testament we find this reference in Psalm 24:1: "The earth is the Lord's and the fulness thereof, the world and they that dwell therein," quoted by the apostle Paul in his epistles. He acknowledged it as God's principle. We have talked about the earth and the fulness thereof, the fruitfulness thereof, now note "the world and they that dwell therein." They belong to God, too. In 1 Corinthians 6:19–20 Paul said, "Know ye not . . . that ye are not your own. For ye are bought with a price." Peter tells that that price is not corruptable things such as silver and gold, but the precious blood of Jesus Christ. Paul goes on to say, "Therefore, glorify God in your body, and in your spirit which are the Lord's." This is stewardship. He was talking about blood redemption. Saved by the blood, when he said you are bought with a price. Paul said that a man's body was bought with the blood of Christ every bit as much as his soul was. What then of the careless living of professing Christians in the sense of body cleanliness, and body holiness, and body purity and health? Is there a stewardship obligation here, to take care of our bodies? In that same context Paul spoke about the body being the temple of the Holy Spirit. Would you expect the Holy Spirit to dwell within an unredeemed temple? an undedicated temple? an unpurified temple? He dwells within a temple that has been purchased and cleansed by the blood of Christ, cleansed of all sins, and he dwells there in fellowship with a redeemed spirit of man. Our bodies are a house, a temple, in which two people live. Us and God. And we will never be alone for he will be with us forever. He will be with us in our house and then one day we will be with him in his. But we will never be alone.

There's the stewardship of man as well as possessions. Because man is always a steward of everything that he has under his dominion which involves not only the fields, the gardens, and so forth but involves also his control over his own life, even his body. What shall I do with my hands, what shall I do with my voice? My favorite hymn in regard to this subject is that one of Frances Havergal "Take My Life, and Let It Be," Frances Havergal wrote a book entitled, *Kept for the Master's Use.* It is her interpretation of the hymn that we know as "Take My Life and Let It Be." "Kept for the Master's use," my hands, my feet, my voice, my very will because this is the position I'm in. My life cannot be kept for my use because that would be to misappropriate it.

As we view stewardship in its practical application in our churches, to avoid the pitfall of fund raising as if it were an end in itself, or even any sort of objective really titled stewardship, I think we should recognize that God is concerned with people. He's not only concerned about the salvation of the lost man who has never heard, which gives us the missionary incentive for giving, but he is also concerned about the steward, and this may well be his primary concern at this point as far as stewardship is concerned. So if the silver and the gold and the cattle upon the thousand hills are all God's, why didn't he devise some other plan for the redemption of a lost world than to make it subject to willingness of people like you and like me and our members? We readily admit that the mission program is strictly limited by the stewardship response of the people in the pews. Why did God subject the very salvation of human souls to such a capricious thing as this? I can only find one reason in all my Bible study and that is that God is concerned not only with the salvation of the lost man but is also concerned about the spiritual maturity of the steward.

God doesn't want you and me to be covetous. This is idolatry, Paul says. Covetousness is idolatry and the only preventive to covetousness is giving by the love of God in our hearts. Unless our redemption involves the giving of the "love of God in our hearts by the Holy Ghost," there is no hope, we are going to be covetous.

God or Gardener?

But back to the Garden of Eden. Covetousness of the forbidden fruit instead of stewardship. It wasn't the woman's. It was God's.

He reserved it for himself. Actually, at this point she wanted the prerogatives that go with being God instead of the limitations that go with being a gardener. I believe that somehow we are going to have to recognize that this is the root of all sin. Paul said that the love of money is the root of all evil. Is this not covetousness, which in another place he said was idolatry which is worshiping the wrong God? When one is covetous, which God is he worshiping? Is he not elevating himself to say this is mine if I can get it? It's mine if I can take it. Sin after all, is the outgrowth of the contest of the gods and it comes right back to the question, a theological question, what is man, God or gardener? This is the point of sin. This is where man is lost. And this is where the world of people and things is lost and needs to be reconciled through the finished work of our Lord and Savior, Jesus Christ.

2.
Stewardship Is Personal—
God's Concern Is People

Biblical stewardship is basicly theological because of its dealing with man's stewardship relationship to God. It recognizes God's ownership because of his creation and recognizes the fact (Gen. 2:15) that God's plan was to put man in the garden to keep it for him and that this has been man's place in the world from the creation until today. Stewardship is not only theological, it is personal. Now by this personal emphasis I mean that God's plan of stewardship is man-centered. Man's viewpoint of his stewardship should be God-centered. But I am looking at it from the biblical viewpoint here that God's plan, from God's view of the plan, is man-centered. To introduce this thought let me make a few basic statements.

God's Concern Is for Man

Jesus has declared the worth of man. For example, in the Sermon on the Mount, Matthew 6:25–30, Jesus pointed out that a man's life is of more importance than his food. His body is of more importance than the clothing that he wears. Man is of more worth to God than sparrows and yet even a sparrow does not fall from the heavens without the knowledge of the heavenly Father. Now with this concept of the worth of man as declared by Jesus, we move to a second step and realize that God has been planning for the worth and the development of man all along. For example, in Mark 2:27 Jesus pointed out that even the sabbath had been established for man, not man for the sabbath. In the Ten Commandments God was not setting up laws to be kept. He was setting up laws and rules, restrictions of discipline for the development of man. Jesus makes this clear specifically in relation to the sabbath. God was not concerned about designating holy days for the sake of having holy days, but he knew that a man who works and labors seven days a week burns out. Scientifically, the physicist tells us, that even our material world is geared to a six-day week. A piece of machinery, if you clock the hours of its operation this physicist declared, will operate fewer total hours if it is run constantly day and night seven days a week than if it is allowed to rest one day out of seven.

The men in the timberlands know that a log chain will break sooner if it is put under strain constantly seven days a week than if it is left to lie idle on the ground one day a week. The metals in the chain, the metals in the machinery came out of the dust of the earth, just as did man. And all of God's creation is geared for a week that recognizes one day because man, like the log chain and the machinery, will break down if he does not take care of the inner man, at least one seventh of the time. The sabbath was made because man needs one day out of seven, not because God needs to have a holy day.

Now this teaching of our Lord is itself, I believe, a declaration that God's concern is for man. Stewardship, I repeat, is not a scheme for raising funds. Stewardship is not a financial program. Stewardship in the Bible is a program of development of God's children. The apostle Paul declared in 1 Corinthians 10:11 that all of what happened and is recorded in the Old Testament happened for our example and it was recorded for our admonition.

In a discussion with one of our members, we came to understanding and agreement that our experiences, even our adverse experiences as Christians, have their purpose and their value in preparing us for what God expects of us tomorrow. Some things you and I would not be able to do tomorrow, if we did not have tears today. If you and I did not get our hearts broken once in a while in our own personal lives, we wouldn't know how to weep with those who weep. Paul said even the experiences of God's people in Israel were for the same reason—that we could learn by the experience of others as well as ourselves, and they are recorded for our admonition. That's why he wrote it down. God did not cover up the sin of David. He covered it with the blood so far as judgment is concerned, but in the record it is there in all of its horror because he wanted you and me to learn from David's experience that these things can lead only to repentance and sorrow. Now all of this then points to the fact that even the writing of the Bible was for the blessing of man, not for the sake of preserving God's holy record. God's whole scheme, even his scheme of redemption, is man-centered.

God is concerned about us. Paul likewise stated in Ephesians 4:11–12 that pastors and evangelists and teachers were given to the churches for the perfecting of the saints. This is God's purpose all along. Again, it was so declared and determined by God, as Paul records for us in the eighth chapter of Romans, along with such profound doctrines as justification and predestination, He says that both of these are for the ultimate purpose of "conforming us to the image of God's son." If you'll put that verse as the key verse of Romans 8 and read the chapter, I think you'll find some light that we may have missed as we gloried in the assurances of the chapter. There are great assurances of our faith in the eighth chapter of Romans but I believe verse 29 is the key to the whole thing, that he has predestined the justified to be conformed to the image of his Son. That's the reason nothing can separate us from the love of God, because God isn't through with us yet. God is growing us. This is what stewardship is all about, too. In the preceding verse, Romans 8:28, we read, "all things work together for good to them that love God, to them who are the called according to his purpose." This puts us into the purpose of God. If you'll allow me to paraphrase, everything is made to contribute to this end and therefore it is good. Every experience of your life and mine is made to contribute to our conformation to the image of the Son of God; to our spiritual maturity toward the stature of the fulness of Christ, as Paul phrased it in Ephesians 4:12. These things then all fit together and we must see that stewardship is just one more facet, man's position between God and the material world, which is a part of stewardship, and man's position between God and his own God-given talents. We are stewards of our talents. We are stewards of our opportunities. As pastors we are stewards of crises. The crises that come in the lives of our people, we are God's man to help them make this to contribute to the end of their conformation to the image of Jesus, therefore to the maturity of that individual Christian. Our own crises and the crises of our people are all a part of our stewardship.

We know of course from the Scriptures also that we are stewards of the gospel, "stewards of the manifold misteries of God." All of these things are a part of our responsibility as individual Christians so the whole breadth of stewardship is really the position of man in God's program and God's program is really set for the development of the man toward the stature of the fulness of Christ, toward conformation to the image of Christ, to the spiritual maturity of that individual believer.

Stewardship Proves the Man

Now, with this foundation that God's concern is for man, I want to consider this question of stewardship of material things. Let me share with you a little story. To me it is the simplest little illustration of what stewardship is all about. It's not original with me at all but my good friend W. H. Allison in Missouri, told this a good many times in my hearing. A farmer had two sons and in the rural community where they lived it was customary that on Saturday afternoon everybody went to town. The women did the shopping and the men did the gossiping. This one man, however, with his two sons, didn't enter into this. They worked in the fields until sundown just like they did any other day and then he did his shopping in the evening. As he came into town one Saturday evening, one of his neighbors stopped him and said, "I've been meaning to talk to you about your habit of working on Saturday afternoon." He said, "I noticed today as we came to town that your boys were working in the corn fields when all the rest of the young people were in town having a good time. The men were visiting, the women were shopping, but the young people were having a good time together. Your boys miss out on it every week." He said, "I just don't understand why you do this to your boys." He said, "surely you can do as well as the rest of us and you can raise corn without working your boys on Saturday afternoon." The man replied, "Well, I'll tell you neighbor, the problem is not a matter of raising corn without working on Saturday afternoon. You see, I'm not raising corn, I'm raising boys. And I can raise better boys teaching them to work than I can just turning them loose to play."

Now if we would take this simple little story and apply it here and realize that in this business of a Christian ministry our task as pastors is raising Christians, not money. If we raise the right kind of Christians, God through those mature Christians will provide the material needs for everything and anything that he intends for the church to do. Money is no problem. People are the problem and our task is perfecting the saints, our task is maturing the Christians—turning the babes into men.

Turn to 2 Corinthians 8:1–12. There are a good many passages that could be used, of course, but I find three very distinctive points in 2 Corinthians 8 that I want to use for this study. Let's look at some of these verses individually, beginning with verse one of 2 Corinthians 8. Going back to the beginning, let's remember that Paul's concern here was the matter of a special offering for the poverty stricken saints in Jerusalem. In the first letter to the Corinthians he explained to them how the offering should be taken. In the first verse of 1 Corinthians 16 he pointed out that he had given the same instructions to all the churches of Galatia and then in the second verse he explained to them that it should be done weekly, it should be done regularly, it should be done proportionately, and with that background of the offering and the plans that had been made, as he says here, "a year ago," he comes now to say some more things about it.

In his appeal for this offering he does not indicate that he made a chart of a thermometer that would allow the red to rise as the money came in. This might be a good visual aid but he was not talking about visual aids. I think the reason that he wasn't in this particular passage was that Paul was not really as concerned about the offering for the saints in Jerusalem as he was the benefit of the offering spiritually for the saints in Corinth. Notice that he emphasized concerning the contribution from the Christians in Macedonia for the same offering that he said "they first gave their own selves." This should always be the pattern. Stewardship is man-centered in God's program. And our giving financially in dollars and cents should really be a testimony of our personal dedication.

I personally believe that the tithe is not strictly a percentage program for the means of underwriting a budget. I believe that the tithe in the Bible is simply the testimony, it is the sign of the dedicated steward, just as circumcision was the sign of the Jew, and without it he couldn't be a Jew. He might have been born of the lineage of Abraham but until he was circumcised he wasn't counted a part of the covenant family. Baptism is a sign of the committed Christian. You can profess faith in Christ with your lips, but I think all of us are reticent and questioning concerning the faith of a man who says, "I'm a Christian but I have never been baptized." Why? Where is the sign of his public commitment? Tithing stands in the same position, I believe, so far as stewardship is concerned. You know your own reaction when a man says, "well, I don't tithe because God owns everything and he owns all I have and I just want to use it all for God." He means he doesn't want the church to use 10 percent of it for God. You question that man's stewardship, don't you? Of course you do. The man who talks in glowing terms about his dedication but hasn't performed the public sign of it is like the unbaptized Christian and the uncircumcised Jew. There's something lacking. God will have to judge his heart, we can only look at the outside. Jesus told us that we couldn't be judges but we could be fruit inspectors and "by their fruits ye shall know them." I question the dedication of a man who is not a tither. Not because he has to give 10 percent of his money to be dedicated, but because, if he is dedicated, his public declaration of it is his open commitment as a tither in relation to his material possessions. Now as we come to this, Paul says, "They first gave their own selves." Brethren, you can't do anything else. Money is nothing but cold cash unless the heartbeat is there first. This is what makes stewardship live—when it starts with the life. You will not need to be concerned about where the money will go if the life is already committed.

I would like to also say in this regard that I believe this offering of which Paul was writing was over and above the tithe. Paul was not appealing to these Christians in Corinth to become tithers. I think Paul with his Pharisaical background would have been the first to have taught tithing if he hadn't already gotten it done when he was there. The pattern of tithing, the proportional concept of tithing, was declared in his first epistle, even in regard to special offerings. He declares the proportionate concept in this passage when he says, "It is according to what a man has, not according to what he has not." So that our giving is to be on a proportionate basis the same as our tithing. But he is talking about an offering here. Malachi declares to us that we can rob God not only in tithes but in offerings. He says, "tithes *and* offerings" (Mal. 3:8). This is God's plan and I think we are not straining the Scriptures at all to say that a man has not really given until he has gone beyond the tithe. This is the realm in which Christians ought always to live. It's comparable to the second mile and the second cheek. It's a matter of dedication. It's not a matter of law but a matter of dedication. I believe at this point we make a mistake today as Southern Baptists, if I might be critical of our Baptist family. We hear so much chatter concerning the Cooperative Program versus special offerings. This is no problem except to the penny-pinching Baptist that does not want to do what he is capable of doing in a program of world missions. A special offering has never hurt the Cooperative Program on the part of people who understand Bible stewardship. It's not a question of either/or, it's both/and. I have declared more than once to our own congregation, that if all of the missionaries that were needed to evangelize the world were on the field, if all the hospitals that were needed were built and staffed, if all the educational institutions were built and staffed, and all the program of both Foreign and Home Mission Boards were under-written with proper necessary needed endowments through the Baptist foundations I'd still be for taking an offering. If the mission fields didn't need a dime, there isn't a member in my church that doesn't need the giving. I thank God the needs aren't met yet because people need that challenge. When somebody says to me, "Now let's stop this special offering business and just give it week by week and give it percentagewise to the Cooperative Program," he reminds me of the Baptist that sits down once a month and writes a check to the church for the whole family and doesn't put either a dime or an envelope into the plate for a whole month. He's putting God on the same par with the water bill, and my church is not a utility, nor is it a charity. It's something that demands the dedication of life. And brethren, if we drift into these poor steward-ship habits we're going to answer to God for it. We need to lead our people to spiritual maturity and realize that we need the week-by-week giving. I would gear the church budget and the Coopera-tive Program to the tithing habits of our people week by week, but if every member of my church were tithing every Sunday morning, I'd still want to take an occasional offering in order to get them to get down and dig and make some sacrifices for God and God's work. Now, that's just the conviction of one preacher, but I believe that it's right here in this eighth chapter of 2 Corinthians. I believe that's what Paul was talking about.

Now notice some verses. Verse 7 says, "Therefore, as ye abound in every thing, in faith and utterance" and knowledge and diligence. . . ." You have what Williams in his translation calls "enthusiasm." Really, the world that's translated "diligence" here, according to my lexicon indicates that the Greek word is "spoudē" which is related to our English word "speed." You can see that in the concept of the diligence that gets at it hastily. David said, "the Lord's work requires haste." Paul says to these Christians in Corinth, even though you had all the diligent haste about the business of God and you loved us, I wish you would abound in this matter of giving also. "In this grace also." I would like to highly recommend to every one of you *The Grace of Giving.* It's one of the richest study course books you'll find. The grace of giving—we're performing a grace for God when we give. That's like doing God a favor when you come to church on Sunday morning? God is doing you a privilege in allowing you to give.

Some people may have had a point when they have said characteristicly that God can save the heathen without either you or me. I suspect he could, except he didn't plan to do it that way. Jesus didn't understand it was going to be done that way or he wouldn't have given the Great Commission. I find that Paul makes mention of the "unspeakable gift" of being able to participate in offerings and in the preaching of the gospel of Christ. And here he speaks of the grace of giving. It is a grace that God permits you and me to be channels of blessing to other people's needs, both material and spiritual. It is the grace of giving. Peter says that we should "grow in grace and the knowledge of our Lord." I believe that we should recognize that this grace of liberality is a part of a gracious person. It is the outgoing and giving of self, the gracious individual is the one that is "in honor preferring others." The gracious person is the one that is more concerned about meeting the needs and providing happiness for somebody else than for himself and his own happiness becomes the by-product of that of others. Here is the gracious Christian who has learned to give. Charles Welborn told the story some years ago on the "Baptist Hour" of a pastor who wrote a letter to one of his laymen appealing to him in his affluence to participate in a financial need. He got a letter back from the man rejecting the appeal and saying: "It seems to me that you preachers have come to interpret Christianity as give, give, give." The pastor replied to that letter and said: "I thank you for the finest interpretation of Christianity I've ever heard. It is give, give, give. It seems to have begun at Calvary when God gave his Son for us." The grace of giving.

Then, in verse 8 Paul says that it is an, "occasion for the proving of the sincerity of your love." The example of others is a challenge for this. "I speak not by commandment." You can't command or coerce people to give. That's robbery. But "by the occasion of the forwardness of others and to prove the sincerity of your love." Paul, interestingly enough, used the churches of Macedonia and the church of Corinth to challenge each other. That's the first competition. Now people say: "Well I don't want any competition. We don't want any contest or anything of this sort." Well, here it is right here in its finest sense because Paul told the churches of Macedonia what the church in Corinth had pledged to this offering a year ago. So the churches in Macedonia were challenged to do something they could do as well as the church in Corinth. They weren't going to be outdone so they gave sacrificially. Then between the time of the pledge in Corinth and the collection in Corinth, Paul wrote them a letter and this is it. Notice the ninth chapter, he says, "for as touching the ministering to the saints, it is superfluous for me to write to you," but I notice he went ahead and did it anyway. "I know the forwardness of your mind for which I boast of you to them of Macedonia that Achaia was ready a year ago; and your zeal hath provoked very many." It worked! It challenged them. "Yet have I sent the brethren, lest our boasting of you should be in vain in this behalf; that, as I said, ye may be ready." (I told them you were, but I want to be sure you are). "Lest haply if they of Macedonia come with me," (and find out you really weren't ready, then I'm made out to be a liar), "and find you unprepared, we (that we say not, ye) should be ashamed in this same confident boasting. Therefore I thought it necessary to exhort the brethren, that they would go before unto you, and make up beforehand your bounty, whereof ye had notice before, that the same might be ready, as a matter of bounty," (that is of graciousness) "and not as of covetousness." Do you see the competition? Do you see the pressure?

Let me just refer you quickly to the fifth chapter of Acts. In the last few verses of the fourth chapter of Acts we find the record of the giving of the people in Jerusalem in the midst of poverty. You remember the unemployment because so many Jews had become Christians. The Jews didn't employ Christians in those days so they were out of work after Pentecost. They got fired for their religion. Some of them were strangers that were stranded there that could not go back home because of religion. They'd been converted in Jerusalem. In the midst of this material need, we are told that many of the people in the church sold their houses and their lands and laid the money at the apostle's feet; Barnabas is mentioned specifically as one. In the fifth chapter we find that Ananias and Sapphira said: "We can't be outgiven by these other folks. We'll do the same thing. We'll sell our farm and we'll give the money also." And you remember when Ananias brought it in and laid it down, Peter said: "Is that all you got from that farm? Why I thought it was worth at least $1,000 an acre." "Well, that's all there is of it," Ananias said. Peter said, "You're lying. You know you got more than that." And Ananias dropped dead right there. Aren't you glad God doesn't do that in the twentieth century? We wouldn't have time for the funerals for those that don't pay their pledges! Peter came in and he said, "Sapphira, here's the money Ananias left here. He said that's all he got from the farm. Is that really all you got?" She said, "Yes, that's all." She didn't even take time to count. Peter said: "You are lying, too. Who told you you could lie to the Holy Spirit?" Can't you just hear her saying, "Well, who made a pledge to the Holy Spirit anyway? I signed a pledge just because you are having a pledge march in your auditorium, and Barnabas was leading the way and we are just as good as he is and I can give just as much as he can. It may not be all the money that we got for the farm, but it is more than Barnabas gave." She dropped dead and they took her out and buried her too. You see people are challenged by what other people are giving and our response to it is a proving of the sincerity of our love. If Ananias and Sapphira had been sincere in their love, they would have given all of it as they said they were going to.

Now I understand that there are some extenuating circumstances that may make it impossible for a man to keep a pledge. He may pledge on the basis of a crop that doesn't come through, but he and God know that then. But when a man makes a promise to God and does not intend to keep it, or he could keep it, but he changes his mind, the Bible says even in the Old Testament it would have been better not to have vowed it than to have made the vow and not kept it. It is the sincerity of our love that is being tested in our stewardship. You can give without loving, someone has said, but you cannot love without giving. "For God so loved the world that he gave." And if I understand about the language, when he said God "so loved," he was not talking about quantity. He was taking about quality. They had more than one word for love. John 3:16 does not use the word that speaks of filial love or a physical love. He used that special word for love that is used throughout the New Testament to refer to Christian love. The kind of love that cannot be expressed in words, but only in deeds and especially in sacrifices. You can tell your wife every night, "I love you," but she may end up doubting you unless sometimes that love finds expression in action.

God in Christ "loved the church and gave himself for it." That's love. "God so loved the world *that he gave* his only son." That's love. That's the kind of love that Paul was talking about to the Corinthians when he said this offering's going to prove whether you have that kind of love or not sincerely; or if you are filling it in with wax to make it look pretty by your promises. But your performance is essential to true love and this will prove the sincerity of your love. Your sacrifice will prove the sincerity of your love.

Let me remind you at this point that we are dealing with the maturity of Christians and a mature Christian must be mature in grace and in love. Above everything else, this is a part of his spiritual character of Christ-likeness. He must grow in grace and in knowledge of his Lord. He must abound, be overflowing in this grace also, the grace of giving. God planned it this way because he will never be the outgoing person that he ought to be towards other persons until he can learn through the object lessons of material stewardship to give. There are not many people who have learned how to give themselves to other's needs until they have learned to give of their possessions to other's needs. If Christians are going to give Christ to the world because we have him already in our hearts, we are going to have to learn how to do it materially as well as spiritually. It's not enough to say "God bless the missionaries."

James had a few things to say, as well as John, about those people who say "God bless you" to the hungry and the naked, and give them no food. That kind of faith without works is dead. The prayers on behalf of missionaries that are not matched with the giving of the life and the possessions of the man at home is, I believe, a stench to the nostrils of God as much as the sacrifices of the Old Testament were described in God's word. They were made by the people whose lips praised God but in their hearts were far from him. This is a stewardship problem. It is a spiritual problem. It is a personal problem. We must have grace and love together.

Then Paul points out to them in verses 10–12 that there must also be in the stewardship development of the man honesty in commitments. I have already touched on this somewhat, but notice what he says. "And herein I give my advice for this is expedient for you who have begun before not only to do but also to be forward a year ago. Now therefore, perform the doing of it that as there was a readiness to will, so there may be a performance also out of that which you have."

Some years ago a company came out with a sales slogan for their products. I remember that they printed it on a little cellophane decal that could be pasted up. I got one, took it back to the church office and stuck it up on the wall above the secretary's desk. It read, "its performance that counts." She didn't appreciate that too much. It is performance that counts. Paul said the same thing to the Corinthian Christians nineteen hundred years ago. It's performance that counts. You can't feed the hungry saints in Jerusalem with pledges. The pledges have their place. This is the time that the Christian assesses his assets and evaluates his abilities and determines his intentions. But if he stops there, his love is insincere, his grace is insufficient and the people starve to death. It's performance that counts. So he says, "therefore perform the doing of it." I would point out to you that this church made a pledge.

Every once in a while we find people who say, "I don't believe in making pledges." I tell you that if we didn't make pledges we would have more bachelors and old maids than this world would know what to do with. Besides that, I would have two more bicycles at my house and no automobiles. I have three bicycles now, one for each boy. I'd have to get one for myself and one for my wife. We would have no automobile because I've never bought one except with a pledge. Have you? We buy automobiles, we connect utilities in our homes, we enter into marriage, all sorts of things by pledges. Our society, our economics today is on the basis of credit—which is pledges. A man in this day and age who says, "I don't believe in making pledges," is either ignorant or insincere. In either case we need to deal with him spiritually as a Christian.

I believe Jacob made a pledge that night alone with God. He realized that God had some things planned for his life when God announced what he was going to do. Someone asked me one time, "Do you think it was right for Jacob to bargain with God?" Jacob didn't bargain with God. God had already said what he was going to do, and Jacob said, "If God is going to do this which he has said he is going to, then I will surely give him a tenth of all that he giveth me." And he didn't settle that alone quietly out there on the hillside that dark night at the foot of the ladder. But when he arose the next morning he took the very stone upon which he slept during the night and set it up as a pillar, as a monument, if you please, so that every stranger who ever passed by would be able to say, this is Bethel. This is the place where Jacob met God, where he came as a sinner and walked away in cooperation with God as a steward with a tithe as a sign of his covenant. There stands the marker for the day when Abraham's grandson became a tither like his grandfather. From that day to this, we have had pledge cards. I don't care whether you want to carve it on a stone, or write it on a card, but men have been making public commitments to God all these years.

A mature Christian would not fail in the honesty of his commitments. Paul saw that these Christians in Corinth needed not only to grow in grace and prove their love, but they needed also to be honest in their commitments. We must lead our Christian people to be honest in the fulfilment of their responsibilities. I said to my teen-age boy the other day when school was out, "You've got some things you want to do this summer, but if there is any way in the world that you can find yourself a job, even part time this summer, I want you to get one. Not just for the sake of the money, I'm able to provide for you as far as money is concerned. You need a job." I wasn't sitting around the house when I was fifteen I assure you. And I believe that my boy will be a better boy if he can be taught at fifteen the meaning of responsibility and of answering to somebody besides his father. I believe this. I think it is my responsibility as a father to bring him up in this kind of discipline, and to help him and to encourage him to assume responsibility and to follow through with that responsibility. I have the same obligation to my church members, in their spiritual responsibilities. And I believe that was what Paul was talking about when he said, "Now therefore perform the doing of it." Fulfil your responsibilities. You have talked about it but there is going to be something lacking in you if you don't live up to your commitments. You are going to lose your own self respect and you will not be the man that God wants you to be.

This Is for Our Account

In the fourteenth chapter of Romans we notice that Paul said to them that we are going to make a stewardship report. "You are not to judge another man's servant, he says" (see Rom. 14:4). And in Romans 14:12 he says, "Every one of us shall give account of himself to God." In the context it is the report of a servant to his master. You and I are going to make a stewardship report to God. In the fourth chapter of Paul's letter to the Philippians, verses 15–18, he thanked them for their giving to him. They supported him while he was preaching in Corinth. Paul had to apologize to the church in Corinth because he supported himself by the making of tents instead of expecting them to support him financially. Incidentally, I think this is not disconnected from the fact that he had to write them two letters in order to teach them how to give. He had failed to give them his teaching of responsibility when he was there. He didn't put any responsibility on them. I know in starting new work new pastors have to partially support themselves financially. I am not criticizing the pastor in the face of the need. When you are the first Christian in town, there are no Christians to support you. And that was Paul's problem at Corinth. But he organized a church before he left, and I question the advisability of organizing a church that cannot even support its pastor. My father used to say that Christians were just as good as Jews. Ten

Jewish men will have a synagogue and the rabbi will live just as good as any one of the ten, because the tithes of the ten will give him an average income. Christians can do as well. That was the stewardship instructions from my father and I believe it to this day. Paul wrote this to these Philippian Christians, and I remind you that they were part of the Macedonian Christians that were commended so highly in 2 Corinthians 8. What did he say to them? He said, "I say this not because I needed your gift." He did. He was in prison when he got part of it. But he said, "I do it because I desire fruit that may abound to your account." I want God to have the record that you gave it. I could starve to death, but that's between me and God. What a tragedy it would be for you to face God and the record that you had never learned to give. He said, "I wanted it to abound to your record."

God's plan of stewardship reveals and reflects his concern for man and it reflects the fact that even stewardship of material things, though it meets material needs, the whole purpose of it is the development of stewards. God can feed the hungry directly. He did the Jews in the wilderness. He made the birds to fall when they needed it. God could provide anything he wanted to for anybody anywhere; even the gospel without a missionary. But you and I would never grow up if he didn't do it through us. And this I believe is what stewardship is all about.

3.
Stewardship Is Ecclesiastical—
Church-Centered

Stewardship is theological. It is based on our Christian understanding of the nature of God, the nature of man, and the relationship of man in God's world. In the very beginning God put man in the garden to tend it for him and from that time to now, he has been a gardener caring for God's business. Man's problems arise when he tries to act like God instead of a gardener.

Stewardship is personal. God is presenting to us in the Bible stewardship as man-centered. God is more concerned about man than he is the money. In our concept of stewardship we have to be God-centered, because of our understandig that it is in relationship to God. But God's primary concern is the development of the Christian, not the raising of funds, as Paul said concerning the matter of sacrifices, "It is not as if God hath need of anything." We overlook this many times, I think, in our stewardship emphases. We are a little inclined to challenge people to give because of the need. The need is there but I personally feel, in my study of the Scriptures and in my personal experience as a pastor, that this is not the greatest motive for giving. But rather, our concept of our relationship to God and our personal dedication to God is the greatest reason for giving. So that even in our relationship to God, we give because of love, not because of need or because of law.

There is a third facet of the matter of stewardship. Stewardship is ecclesiastical. There might be better words, but it goes best with theological and personal. We understand the word "ecclesiastical" as meaning that it is related to the church. And the thesis that I would like to share with you is that from the Christian viewpoint our stewardship is church-centered. Now if we were talking about tithing, as such, I suppose we would come to use the time-worn expression of "storehouse tithing." I believe it and I practice it. But in all this study of stewardship I have not been talking about tithing. It is a vital part of the practice of stewardship. It is my personal conviction that tithing is a public declaration of our stewardship commitment. I personally like to compare it to the practice of circumcision as the public sign of the Hebrew's commitment to his God and of baptism as the public symbol of the Christian's commitment to God in salvation. When a Christian comes to understand his stewardship relationship to God, the scriptural symbol of that commitment is tithing. I believe one illustration of this is found in Jacob. God said nothing to him about tithing, but he did talk to him that night about his participation in the covenant relationship that God had had with his father and his grandfather. This covenant was to be continued and God's blessing was going to be upon him materially and otherwise. In his response Jacob said, "if God is going to do all of this, then surely I will give him the tenth of all that he gives to me." Undoubtedly he had been taught the principle of tithing from his grandfather and his father, but the thing of interest to me is that this was a response to God's restatement of the covenant. And as he entered into covenant with God in regard to God's plan of world redemption, he gave tithing as his personal commitment as a sign of participation in that covenant. I believe that this is a good pattern for us to follow as Christians.

Now then, when we come not only to the matter of tithing, but to the stewardship of our lives, not only the 10 percent, but the 100 percent, not only the regularity of the tithe on the Lord's day,

but also the matter of offerings, the whole field of material stewardship and the spiritual stewardship, I believe is centered in the
church. I believe this is the greatest place. I remember reading a
quotation from George W. Truett that the church is the greatest
place for man to invest his life for God. I believe that as we preach
this and teach this, it will please our Lord. He loved the church
enough to die for it, and I believe the people who profess to believe
in him should love it enough to join it. And those who profess to
be a part of it should love him enough to support it with their time,
their talents, and their treasures.

Now when we try to establish scripturally that the church is in
the center, that the church is the vehicle of Christian stewardship,
there are several things we may need to set forth as basic to the
concept. As we go into the Old Testament for the background of
our faith and our relationship to God, I find that Abraham, when
it came time for him to demonstrate his continued commitment
to God in covenant, did not take the tenth and use it to suit himself.
He did not build a building to memorialize his own name. He did
not send our missionaries to perpetuate his own testimony. But he
took the "tithe of it all," the Scriptures say, and gave it to Melchizedek. Now some might think all that means is you ought to
give it to the preacher. I've known some places where that was the
pattern. In fact, I grew up in that kind of situation. My father was
the preacher in many cases where that took place because he was
preaching in rural communities and in schoolhouses and in that
sort of thing where there was no church and those who responded
with any concept of tithing at all would have had no place to have
left it except to have given it to the preacher who was preaching
to them. I will admit that I have mixed emotions. I realize that
it was the pattern in much of my childhood and in the ministry
of my father, and yet I have personally come to the conviction that
it is not exactly the New Testament pattern. But it is the case with
Abraham.

However, as we follow through with the Old Testament, the time when there came into being an established center for the people of God as the tabernacle came to be the symbol of God's presence among his people and later the Temple was constructed, we find that his place of worship came to be the place and time when the public practice of stewardship took place. Then of course we come to that most obvious and most familiar passage in Malachi 3:10 when we find him saying, "Bring ye all the tithes into the storehouse." Now I have had some very good Baptist brethren argue with me that we don't have a storehouse anymore. Perhaps not, but Paul had something in mind along that line when he said to the Christians in Corinth to "lay it by in store as God has prospered us." There was some place to put it. There was some intent of it and the fact that he identified it with the first day of the week automatically identifies it with the Christian's concept of worship because that is the Lord's Day. So we find a tithe in here. Stewardship is ecclesiastical (1) in its direction, (2) in its consecration, and (3) in its administration.

In Its Direction

When I say that it is ecclesiastical, meaning church-centered, in its direction, I mean that in the individual's experience of practicing Christian stewardship, he directs it toward the church. As far as the church directing the subject matter of stewardship, we come to that later under the heading of administration and we will see some verses on that. But here I am looking at it from the viewpoint that when Abraham came to practice tithing, the Scripture says in both the Old and the New Testament that he brought those tithes to Melchizedek. And we know that, whatever else professors of today think Melchizedek might have been, he is clearly presented in the New Testament Scriptures as a type of Christ. And there Abraham took the tithes. Then we come to the prophet Malachi and we find him saying, "Bring ye all the tithes into the storehouse that there may be meat in mine house." I think we can take God rather literally at this point. We know of course that they literally had a storehouse. We know that their tithes were coming out of the harvesttime. We know that everything from the fruit of the trees and of the field and of the animals and the oil from the olives and all of this sort of thing could be brought and were brought to the Temple as a part of their worship and here it was kept and here it was dedicated and here it was used as God would have it to be used. Whatever else might be involved besides the storehouse concept, the thing I would like to emphasize is the fact that God stated a purpose for it. When we read that passage, about all we ever see is that God promised to open the windows of heaven and pour out blessings that our poor little storehouse would not hold. I think we can take many passages of Scripture and find material prosperity as a fruitage of spiritual obedience. But this, however, is often a fringe benefit. It is not God's direct purpose, at least not as far as Malachi 3:10 is concerned. For Malachi said, "that there might be meat in mine house." In other words, at this point it was God's plan for the support of his house. For meeting such things daily as bread and meat which would have involved the livelihood of both the priests and the Levites, and whatever else might be involved in the operation of the Temple. We can of course with no difficulty at all transfer the same principle to the New Testament and to our own day.

I believe that missions is the business of the church. It is my conviction that the Great Commission was given to the church. The man, whether he's young or old, who feels the call of God upon his life to become involved in God's program of world redemption can best accomplish the fulfilment of his call by the investment of his life through his church, whether he is being sent out by his church or whether he is supporting those who are sent out, through his church. I believe in church-centered missions, and therefore I believe in church-centered stewardship.

I heard a preacher on the radio some few years ago preaching on the subject of stewardship. When he came down to the close of his broadcast, (Up to this point I would have agreed with everything he said. I realize there were some things he left unsaid but I thought what he said was true until he came to the close of it.) making an appeal to the people, he said, "Now you sit down and figure out how much of the tithe you owe to the Lord and then you make out a check and mail it to me." I thought, that is just about as close to blasphemy as a man can get. When one man, even if God called him to preach the gospel, can say in his own name, "put my name on that check which you owe to God," there is something wrong with the concept of stewardship. I believe in church-centered stewardship. I want no checks made out to me but the one that my church makes out to me.

I believe that this is to be a church-centered affair in its direction, pointing out Malachi's position "that there might be meat in my house." The man that takes any other channel in his stewardship is going to have to take the Scriptures and explain to me and I think a little later he will have to explain it to the Lord more fully, as to the basis upon which he has bypassed that which Jesus loved enough to give his life to it. When we bypass the church, whether it is with our tithe or with our talents, we bypass God's plan. When our talents become too big to be used through a church, we best examine our humility. I believe the church is God's institution.

Paul wrote to the Corinthians, giving stewardship principles. (By the way, let me put in this parenthesis, there is a refreshing shock for your heart if you will study the Bible some time by looking at the climaxes in Paul's epistles. Read those great chapters and then read right on into the next one without stopping and see what it does to you. The eighth chapter of Romans for example, we all glory in it, but the very next verse says that he is willing to give up heaven itself and go to hell if it would save one soul that he just got through saying could not be lost again once it was saved. But he says, "I would be willing for that to happen to me, though I know it can't, if my kinsman could be saved." That's after the climax! Consecration comes after the climax. The valley comes after the mountain. And here again in the fifteenth chapter of 1

Corinthians, the tremendous climax of the victory of the resurrection and you just almost hear the hallelujah chorus, "now concerning the collection," that comes after the climax.) "Now concerning the collection for the saints as I have given order *to the churches* of Galatia, even so do ye" (1 Cor. 16:1). I think while we are not taking up a special benevolence offering, I believe the apostle Paul has set down some principles that can serve as guidelines for us. And here is the first one. He did not make personal appeals to individuals as such, at least not in his epistles. He wrote them to the churches. Here he says he has "given instructions to the churches." That's plural, incidentally, the "churches" in Galatia. And now he said in similar manner you do the same thing over in Achaia. In his second letter we find out that he had also told the churches of Macedonia the same thing. Those are the three major areas of Paul's ministry, which means that in virtually all of the areas where Paul had preached the gospel and established churches, he followed right back up on evangelism with stewardship. And through the churches, he was making the appeal of meeting the material needs of the saints who were in famine in Jerusalem. He had given orders *to the churches*. I think this goes along with Malachi 3:10 and the next verse, of "laying by in store," (1 Cor. 16:2). The thing is church-centered.

In Its Consecration

Now then moving into the second verse. It is ecclesiastical or church-centered in its consecration. I personally feel that the bringing of the tithes and the offerings on the Lord's day to the Lord's house is a vital part of our worship. A very inspiring book by Winston Pierce, *Come Let Us Worship,* makes the statement that "worship is gratitude." This is our expression of thanks. This is our expression of praise to God. This is worship. He also points out that worship is giving. You can go back to the Old Testament of course and find that the Jews were forbidden to ever come into the house of God without an offering. They were not to come into the presence of the Lord empty-handed. I think of this as we sing that hymn, "Must I Go and Empty-Handed." The author of the hymn and the message of the hymn is talking about the judgment day in regard to evangelism, that I go without any souls or any trophies for my king. But I think it might be a good hymn to sing as an opening call to worship on Sunday morning sometime. Must I come into the house of the Lord empty-handed? I realize that sometimes we get personally moved by a particular thought and we go to extremes on it. Maybe I've gone to an extreme on this. I don't know how you practice your tithing or whether you do or not. But I have for some twenty years been paid once a month. I have always divided my tithe among the four or five Sundays of the month because when the Lord's day comes, I want to know that on that day I have brought something to my Lord. I believe this, I preach this, and I practice this. I believe 1 Corinthians 16:2; it teaches it. It was to be upon the first day of the week that they were to lay it by in store. I have known men (and I have seen some of them change their ways after I have preached to them for a little while) who sat down once a month and wrote a check out to the church for the whole family, and every member of the family put in empty envelopes for the sake of the Sunday School records for every Sunday of the month. They may have written the word "tithe" or something on it, but the father wrote the check for the whole family just like he wrote the check for the utilities for the home, and probably did it the same night that he wrote out all the other checks. I think this does violence to the spirit of worship. I think this is putting God and the church on too much of a business basis. I think it robs them of something at the hour of worship.

I remember one deacon in particular who was asked to serve as the general director of the Forward Program one year. I confronted him with this. He had three daughters and I had three sons. And I asked him what he was doing to teach his children tithing. He said: "Well, I tithe, and you tithe, and the Sunday School teachers teach tithing and you preach tithing. What more do you want me to do?" And I said, "I want you to teach them to tithe." He said, "Well, how can I do that?" I said, "Do they know that you tithe?" He said, "Yes." I said, "Do they know that you provide food and clothing for the whole family out of the same paycheck?" He said, "Of course, they do." And I said, "Why not let them share in the experience of worship in giving to God, at least to the proportion that they share the clothing and the food of the family? They are a part of the family in everything except in giving to God. And their daddy takes care of it for them. One day they are going to get their own job and one day they are going to be independent and they won't know how even to figure the tithe, as simple as it might be, simply because you never taught them how to figure it or even let them have a part in bringing it." Well, a few days later I knew I had a convert because I overheard him straightening out another deacon on the same point. I believe this. I believe it is something that is a part of our worship. Now if a man gets paid once a month and wants to give his tithe once a month, then I would suggest that he find an offering the other three times. But I personally do not want to come to the Lord's day without feeling that I'm having part in my church today.

Paul said, "Do it on the first day of the week, it's part of worship." You'll notice also the churches were appealed to. He made reference in 2 Corinthians 8:1–5 to the fact that the churches of Macedonia had given sacrificially. Now we know that no church gives more than its members give, for it has no source other than its membership. We know that if a church has made a sacrifice, then its members have been willing to forgo some of its luxuries, comforts, conveniences, or dreams. No church makes a sacrifice that is not preceded by the sacrifice of the individual members. I think some churches corporately may make a whole lot less sacrifice than what its members are willing to make in their own homes. I think sometimes we need to take a look at the family budget and the church budget. There may be some people talking about how the church ought not to have a nice building, we ought to give it all to missions. I always take a look the next time I drive down the street to see if he practices the same principle in regard to his own house. This is scriptural, incidentally. David said, "My God dwelleth in tents while I dwell in a house of cedar." He was willing to compare his own house with God's house. And I think our members might well do this sometimes. But few churches are going to have more spirit of sacrifice budget-wise than what is found in the heart and the experience of the individual members. We need to start here. Paul's appeal was to the church. And he noted the fact that the churches of Macedonia had given sacrificially. I think this is justifiable exposition, to tie them together in a sense of pattern, in that he said that he had appealed to the churches, to participate in this benevolence offering, then we read in that context, he mentioned that it be done on the first day of the week. I think we can see that here was true spiritual worship that resulted in sacrificial giving. I believe they go together. The church that is not able to get in the spirit on the Lord's Day is not likely to have a very sacrificial offering. When we come with sacrificial giving, and because of love for the Lord and concern for the people, in this kind of spirit of giving, I believe is found a most genuine worship.

In Its Administration

Looking at 2 Corinthians, the eighth chapter, beginning with verse four and then verse fourteen, I'd like to point out that in its administration, giving was church-centered. In the fourth verse he says, "Praying us with much intreaty that we would receive the gift, and take upon us the fellowship of the ministering to the saints." The churches of Macedonia had entreated Paul that he would personally deliver the offering to Jerusalem. I think that it is of significance when we look now at this matter of administration of the offering that the church resumed responsibility for its administration.

I had an interesting experience some years ago. Perhaps you have never had anybody criticize the financial operation of your church. But I had it happen at least one time, and I had the privilege of overhearing the answer of a very fine dedicated deacon. One of the members asked him, "Do you agree with the way in which this church is spending our money?" The deacon's answer was this, "It's not our money. It's God's money. While it was in my hands, I was responsible to bring the tithe and the offering to the Lord's house on the Lord's Day." He said, "I did that, I put it in the plate, and that's the end of my responsibility except to cast one vote at the next business meeting. But what happens to that money after it has been placed in the plates is the business of this church as a body, not my business as an individual." I appreciate a deacon like that and I believe he was scriptural. I believe Paul makes it clear in the next few verses that the matter of administration of stewardship is church-centered. Paul said, "The churches asked him to deliver that offering." This is appropriate.

Now turning to verse 14 Paul said: "I mean not that other men be eased, and ye burdened: But by an equality, that now at this time your abundance may be a supply for their want, that their abundance also may be a supply for your want: that there may be equality." I believe that when there is church-centered administration, there is more likelihood of equality, in its administration. I have more confidence in the democratic wisdom of a converted congregation, being Spirit-born. I have more confidence in the whole congregation being Spirit-led than I have in the infallability of any one member of that church, even the preacher. I have confidence in the democratic process and I am willing to wait for it to operate. It's slow, but it's like waiting for the lights to change at intersections. You can get in a hurry and go on across if you want to, but it's a little safer to wait, and democracy is the same way. You can get in a hurry and go right ahead and you may come out with the same results, but it's a little safer to let democracy take its course.

I think I see the Cooperative Program in principle in this passage. Paul was involved in many churches in one project; and not to lay an undue burden on one church in order that another might escape responsibility, but that there might be equality. All of them doing according to the ability that God had given them, meaning that God was blessing them materially. Therefore, God was enabling them to do it.

Perhaps we in our church life ought to back up one step at this point and help our members to understand the reasons for God's blessing in their lives materially.

I remember one particular instance when an unusually large offering came in and someone wanted an explanation for it and another man standing nearby said: "Brother so and so sold a house this last week and this is his tithe of his profit." As if that explains everything. This one man, that is no credit for anybody, no glory to God. One man! And I sensed the tone of voice with which he said it. It was just like you were explaining away a miracle. I said, "Brother, don't overlook the fact that he could have lost money on that house if it hadn't been for God." And God has no way, according to his own providence, to provide the material needs of his churches except through the material prosperity of his people. If this church needs a thousand dollars, one of our farmers is going to have to have a real good cotton crop. Or somebody is going to have to sell a house. God is not going to rain pennies from heaven into the plate on the table.

I believe that our people need to be made aware of the fact that their own closeness to God, so that God can bless them and use them as channels of blessing, is God's way of meeting the needs of his churches. And the same thing is true out there on the mission field. God is going to have to bless our churches, his churches, if he is going to provide five thousand foreign missionaries as the Foreign Mission Board has suggested. He is going to have to bless us with revivals that will result in the commitment of young people to missionary service. Our Mission Board doesn't have any young people, except who come from our churches.

Stewardship of life begins in the churches. When you think in terms of the balance of a world program, of world missions, of world redemption, call it what you like, it is dependent upon what God is able to do through his churches. And that's the people. That's us. Here he says, "that there be equality among the churches."

I want to point out some things of special interest here. In verse 18 he says, "And we have sent with him the brother whose praise is in the gospel throughout all the churches." He's talking now about the men who were traveling from church to church collecting the offering that it might be taken to Jerusalem. They didn't have the mail service that we have today, you know. One of the modern English translations would indicate that the man he is recommending here, whom he doesn't name, was one whose praise is in the preaching of the gospel in the churches. In other words, one of the evangelists was drafted into the stewardship department. Where better to find a man dedicated to the total cause of Christ than the man who has lost souls on his heart? He was effective with the gospel and therefore recommended by the churches.

Notice verse 19, the first group of denominational workers. "And not that only but he was also chosen of the churches to travel." Now it goes on to say some other things, but I think it might be good to stop right there. It's a good Baptist phrase: "Chosen by the churches to travel." That's the first denominational worker. What he says is that they were chosen of the churches to travel with us, with this grace, which is administered by us to the glory of the same Lord and the declaration of your ready mind." There is the word administration. He speaks of the evangelistic background of one brother. In verse 22 he points out the diligence of another. "We have sent with them our brother whom we have oftentimes proved diligent in many things." Williams' Translation of the word diligent is "enthusiastic." Another meaning of the word is "with haste"—a man who wasn't always putting it off until tomorrow. We put it into the hands of somebody who understood the urgency of God's business. That we do it *not*. That was another qualification in this matter of stewardship.

Verse 23 says, "Whether any do inquire of Titus, he is my partner and fellowhelper concerning you: or our brethren be inquired of, they are the messengers of the churches." The churches elected these messengers and the word that is translated messengers is the word for apostle—people who were sent. They were sent by the churches to take care of this offering. I believe it was administered by the churches.

Another interesting note in here is where the word administered appears, Paul uses it twice in this passage. In verse 20, he says, "avoiding this that no man should blame us in this abundance which is administered by us." He used the word administered in another verse (19) and in both places the word that is translated administered is the same basic word that we translate as deacon, which gets us back again to the servant concept in this matter of stewardship. Even these messengers of the churches were in a "deacon" capacity. They were serving as servants of the churches, and the administering of financial affairs was a deacon responsibility. Now if you haven't found a prooftext for it before, here is one you can use, besides the sixth chapter of Acts where they were first selected to wait on the table. A servant capacity. I think it is worthy of note then that these men were chosen by the churches, they were elected, they were messengers, they were sent out by the churches. They were in a servant capacity of the churches to carry out this task.

In all of the matters of stewardship, if you look at it from the viewpoint of the individual Christian, basically, theologically and personally we see his position in relation to God. But when the redeemed Christian begins to demonstrate and to perform his stewardship relationship his proper channel is through the church. That's where his life ought to be if he is going to count for Christ, if he is going to count for the most. Then we find that the responsibility rests upon the church for the receiving of the tithes and the offerings, for the administration of the tithes and offerings, for the sending out of those who are responsible for the performance of this material responsibility, taking the money to its proper place, was a church-administered responsibility.

I think this is a passage that ought to help all of us realize we have a reason to be pleased with our Southern Baptist missionary and stewardship arrangement. As I've already indicated, I believe the basic principle of the Cooperative Program is right here in this chapter, and I don't say that just out of denominational loyalty. If I were looking for a way in which to find a scriptural pattern by which my church could cooperate with other churches in common causes, I believe this chapter presents the pattern. I cannot find anything in operation today closer to it than our Cooperative Program. Each individual church's participation, the limit of its participation, the amount of its participation, is determined by that church. That church decides how much it is going to give. This gets it back where there is personal responsibility in matters of stewardship. Nobody from the outside is telling a church what to do. The church is limited only by the dedication of its own members.

The church is at the center of it, not only for the receiving of the tithes so that the tither can be told where his tithe ought to be brought, but that that church is then also a steward. This is a point that we should preach on occasionally. Churches are stewards too. I remember a church that I pastored a few years ago. I had gone as a new pastor, and one of the deacons, the chairman of the deacons as a matter of fact, was telling me rather proudly one day, "Our church tithes." I said, "Is that right? Would you mind explaining that to me." He said, "Yes, tithing is 10 percent and our church gives 10 percent to missions. We're tithing." And he said it with the sense of pride of having arrived. We've got it made! I said, "I'm sorry but I don't understand what you are talking about because I can't find any place in my Bible where tithing is used in reference to a church, except on the part of the individual Christian bringing his tithe to the church. This I believe. But the church's stewardship of it after receiving it, I do not find any percentage figure of it in the Scripture. If I were to look for a principle, I don't think I would find it limited to 10 percent."

Paul said concerning the stewardship of life, and I think it is applicable in church, "the man that is approved is not the man that commends himself, but the one that is commended of God." I believe that when a church faces up to its stewardship commitments and it's relationship to God's world redemption program, it's going to have to face up to it just as realistically as the man that sits down with his Bible and his checkbook to say "where is my part in this?" Our churches are stewards, too. And that is the sum result of saying that stewardship is ecclesiastical. It is church-centered. Our churches are going to be called upon to be honest with God in the matter of funds received and used in the cause of Christ because it is somebody's tithe.

Stewardship is theological in its rootage. It's personal in its commitment, but it is ecclesiastical in its performance.

4.
Life: Whole or Fractured

There is a tragic condition in our world referred to as schizophrenia, which in layman's language means a split personality. A man who may be a totally respectable citizen and a meaningful person in one set of circumstances, may in another set of circumstances seem virtually the opposite. This is a tragic condition. We frequently find cases coming into the trial courts of our land when crimes have been committed in which lawyers and psychiatrists attempt to prove to the court that the real reason for the crime was a mental condition of schizophrenia.

There is another condition very much like it that may be called spiritual schizophrenia, in which we have allowed our lives to become split. They have been fractured by fractions. We know that we spend more of our time earning money than in any other one thing. Consequently, the money that a man holds in his hand may represent more of his life than would be represented by any other one thing. Yet, what does he do with it? He fractures it. He sets aside a percentage, a tenth, and says that this is sacred. But what he does with the nine tenths may be completely the opposite. Or he looks at his life in terms of time and he fractures it when he says one day out of seven, one-seventh, is sacred. But the six-sevenths may be used for something completely different or totally opposite. A life has been fractured and it is no longer whole. We have tried to put ourselves into compartments, and we have tried to say that this area of life over here has no bearing or relationship on this over here. There are those for example, who have said that religion has nothing to do with business. Some years ago religious controversy raised around a candidate for the presidency of the United States and in the midst of that controversy he said, "My religion will have no bearing whatsoever upon my service as president of the United States." Now I am not going to evaluate his presidency. We will let the historians do that. But I am saying he fractured his life when he said over here is my religion and over here is my public service. Let's not be too hard on the young man. There are many others who do the same thing every week. They just don't have television cameras in front of them when they say it. But they say it to preachers, if not to the public. "You and the church stay out of my business." Or, "You and the church leave politics alone. Religion and politics won't mix." I have heard that false adage all my life, and when I look at some of the politics around, it sure doesn't mix with religion. But that politician whose life is in it is fractured because there is one part of his life that he cannot allow to become mixed with the rest.

We've taken a verse completely out of its context when we've said, "Let not your left hand know your right hand is doing." And we've tried not to let our Sunday suit know where our other clothing goes. We are not wanting to let one dollar know what the other nine are doing. We are not wanting one day of the week to know what the other six are doing. We have fractured our lives. It would take a serious study by the psychiatrists and the theologians together to determine how many of human ills that we are suffering with these days are really attributable to a fractured life. There is no real peace because, you see, the word "peace" itself, in its biblical origin, means a unity—a oneness. A life that is fractured has lost its oneness. It has lost its unity, and tensions build up between the appeals and the pressures and the claims and the commandments of one as over against the claims and the appeals and the pressures of the other. These tensions can rise to such a point that it would seem that our lives will be literally pulled apart. Sometimes it happens and someone says, "Well, he was a religious fanatic." Perhaps so but there are some others that have had the same result because they were political fanatics or business fanatics or pleasure fanatics or home fanatics. Because they became fanatics of any one facet of life and separated it and segregated it from the rest, their life becomes fractured and it never really amounts to much any more. Oh, it may have monetary success in the business segment but it lacks of spiritual power in the religious segment or it may have influence in the political segment but be a reprobate in the spiritual segment. That's the way life appears sometimes.

If you'll read the life and the ministry of Jesus as recorded in the four Gospels of the New Testament, you will find that one of the things that he said many times was that he came to make people whole—to make them whole, so that these fractured lives might be reunited, that these disturbed, distraught, and divided minds might have peace. And that these hearts that are pulled apart with contradictory passions may be united with a single passion.

The Bible has a great deal to say about single-mindedness, single-heartedness, and single-tongued. James tells us that a man who is divided cannot expect to receive anything from God (Jas 1:7). He was talking about prayer when he said that. The fractured life, he was saying, has no power in prayer. Is that why we have so many powerless church members? So many powerless Christians for whom prayer is a ritual, a form, a habit but not a real channel of power to change the world or to even change the circumstances of their own little sphere, because they really don't have a sphere. They have a fractured life and there is no power before God in a fractured life.

There is a verse in the Beatitudes that declared it was the pure in heart who would see God. The word "pure" does not only speak of moral purity but it means the undivided loyalty of a heart. The one whose loyalty is unquestioned has access to his Ruler. The divided life has no power in prayer but the united heart that is single in its loyalty to God has access to his very throne of grace. Life: whole or fractured? You think of yours while I share with you some of the principles of this kind of wholeness of life as we find it in the World of God.

God Is Creator

In the first place we need to recognize that God is the creator of life. Now, if you believe that this world of ours, including ourselves, has come into being because of an accident somewhere, just a happenstance, then you won't believe anything that I am going to say. Bible-believing Christians believe *all* the Bible, including the first eleven chapters of Genesis. Bible-believing Christians believe that Almighty God created this world of ours, not by the splitting of atoms, not by the shattering of planets or the falling of stars, but by the compacting of that which he made to be one, a uni-verse. A universe God made. It's one, not many, and it all relates within itself and to God, the Creator. We must see ourselves as also a creation of God and the Bible declares that we are created in the image of God. Dr. Albert McClellan said, "Faith begins when a man realizes that he is not God." This was part of the sin that took place in the Garden of Eden when the devil said to Eve, "If you'll eat of this fruit you'll be as God, knowing good and evil." Man has always wanted to be god. The man that makes himself god is worshiping himself, not his creator. If you want to have a whole life you'll have to find it in its right relationship to God just as our universe stays together "by the word of his power," the Bible says. It maintains its right relationship to each other as planet to planet and star to star, and all of it within the word of his power. Until your life is brought into this right relationship with God you are going to find yourself fractured with choices and tensions.

God Is Owner

God is our Creator. The Scriptures says, "The earth is the Lord's and the fulness thereof, the world and they that dwell within." This is our Father's world by right of creation. He made it, and it is his. We must recognize that this is God's world. That is the second acknowledgment. It belongs to him. The ownership of God is at the very center of our Christian faith. It is at the center of the record of the Bible from Genesis to Revelation. Not only did God make the world, but God owns the world. You and I may use it, but it never is ours. It's always his. Through the psalmist, God said, "If I were hungry and had need, I would not tell you, for the world is mine." We should ponder that for a while. The church belongs to God. And God said "if I had need, I wouldn't ask you, for the world is mine." Why in this world then are we bringing offerings when we come to worship? If faith begins when man recognizes that he is not God, stewardship begins when a man witnesses to the sovereignty of God by bringing offerings. Paul said to the men in Athens, (not Christians, just preaching to the people in Athens, to the careless quibblers in the marketplace) he spoke of God as the creator of the heavens and the earth, and he declared that he is not one that has need of anything. Again the psalmist tells us that when we come to worship God, we bring to him nothing that is not his own. Why then do we bring it? We bring our offering to God simply as a witness of the sovereignty of God over our lives and in the world.

I heard a story some years ago about a church in the South that had a parking problem. Close by was a supermarket. Believe it or not, it was closed on Sunday. The church inquired of the owner of the supermarket as to whether they could use his parking lot on Sunday. He said: "Yes, you can use our parking lot on Sunday, fifty-one Sundays a year, but not fifty-two. One Sunday a year the entrance to it will be chained off." They inquired why this odd restriction. He said, "I want you never to forget that that parking lot belongs the supermarket, not to the church."

This is why God has made reservations for himself, that we might in stewardship acknowledge the sovereignty of God. He owns that cotton field, he owns that oil well, he owns that fruit orchard, he owns that house you live in, and every baby that you have cradled in it and don't forget it! Don't let it fracture your life, however. Don't think that you can satisfy all your obligations to God with one-tenth of the cotton or one-tenth of the grapefruit or one-tenth of the children, for that matter. No need to think that your parental responsibilities would be fulfilled if you had ten children and one of them became a preacher. God isn't wanting to fracture your family by having just one preacher. He would rather have ten really dedicated Christians, regardless of whether one is in the ministry or not. He wants your whole life, regardless of whether one-tenth of it is designated for the church treasury or not, or whether one-seventh of your time is designated for church attendance. A whole life can grow out of the acknowledgment that we are stewards of it all and that what we give to God, a fraction of the whole, is only a testimony that all of it is sacred.

We have made an error and brought a grave injustice to our own lives when we have founded our concepts of living on the basis that some things are sacred and some things are secular. You don't find that in the Bible at all. You do not find any justification in the Bible for one day being sacred as over against other days. The idea of it all is that one day being set aside would be a testimony of our living all of them for God. And that one-tenth of the money would be set aside, but I'm using it all for the glory of God. But we have fractured our lives by trying to make something sacred in fractions and leaving the rest of it secular, unholy, worldly, fleshly, and materialistic. It doesn't take anything but a first grader to figure out that if one-tenth of your money is sacred, you've got nine times that much that is unholy. If only one-seventh of your time is holy, then you've got six times as much of it that is unholy. It doesn't take long for a life to become totally ungodly with that kind of thinking, fractured thinking as it is. God doesn't ask for your money *or* your life, as the robber; he asks for your money *and* your life. The whole life.

Man Is Steward

Looking into the Scriptures, then, we can find some areas in which we as stewards can demonstrate our stewardship without this fractured way of living. Jesus said in this parable that some were given five talents and some three and some two. We in our English language have misinterpreted this passage a lot of times trying to think, "Now who in the world do I know that has five talents?" But when the King James translation was made, a talent was a piece of money. It was not talking about the word talents as we use it today, as if a man has a talent to speak, a talent to sing, or a talent to do something else. But yet it speaks of both of these, because it was a parable, a parable that points out that we have nothing but what we have received. As Paul said to the Corinthians, "You have nothing but what you have received, wherefore then, do you boast in that which you have, if it was given to you?" And the Bible declares that even the strength to gain wealth is from God. So this parable points out to us that it all came to these servants from their master. Secondly, it points out that they were expected to use these talents, these gifts of money, for the benefit of their Lord, not themselves. And thirdly, there was an accounting to be made they were to return to the Lord that which they had received and that which they had made from it. The man with five talents returned ten. He said, "Lord, here are the five you gave me and here are five more." And that's the kind of accounting you and I are going to face on the judgment day.

Now let's look at the use of these and what are we talking about. Very little of it really has to do with money. Although in our Lord's teachings, as recorded in the Synoptic Gospels, they tell us that six out of every seven verses have to do with man's stewardship of material things. Let's look at man's life as a steward.

First of all, we find in 1 Corinthians, the sixth chapter, that we belong to God, we are not our own, even our bodies and our souls. And in Romans 12 he tells us to present our bodies as living sacrifices unto God. Would you like to fracture your body and give him one finger out of ten? Or would you like to give him one toe out of ten and call yourself a real good Christian, you dedicated something to God? No, he wants your whole body—not a fraction of it. We belong to God.

We find also that our influence is a stewardship. I had conversation with one sometime ago who denied this. He thought our stewardship had to do only with material things, not with our bodies, with our influence, with our time, or with any of these things. And yet I have a whole lot more time than I have money. Most of us have far more influence than we have money. And far more physical strength than we have money. Why not serve God with that of which we have an abundance. Paul said to the Romans, "No man liveth unto himself, and no man dieth unto himself." He said also to the Romans, "Let no man be a stumbling stone in the way of his brother." That's influence. And Paul in dealing with his own Christian influence declared, "If eating meat would cause my brother to be offended, I would eat no more meat so long as the world standeth."

A young man leading a departmental devotional in a Sunday School asked a rather pertinent question at this point when he said, "Do you know anybody who is not a Christian because you are?" Do you know anybody who is not a Christian because you are? That's what Paul was talking about when he said, "Let no man be a stumbling stone to his brother." That's influence. You have a stewardship of influence. It may not be political influence in a community, a state, or a nation. It may be only the influence you have on the maid at your house. It may be the influence you have on a neighbor or the neighbor's children who play with yours, but you have influence. Somebody, somewhere, sometime will make a decision on the basis of what they have seen or heard from you. That's influence. We all have this and we are going to account for it to God. There are times when there are some things we've thought we should leave unsaid. It's odd to me that Baptists, of all people, should brag about their democracy and about their freedom of speech and say by actions and a lot of times in words, "I'll say what I think, no matter what anybody thinks." That's the poorest expression of Christian stewardship I know of. And you will account to God for it. There are some things you had better leave unsaid because of its influence on others, because what you say and the way you say it, what you do and the spirit with which you do it will influence somebody either toward the Lord or away from him. That is stewardship. Our influence should be a testimony of the sovereignty of God. Our whole influence, not a fraction of it.

Our time is the same way, Paul said to the Romans and the Ephesians both, "Redeem the time for the days are evil." Redeem time. How can I redeem time? I cannot buy back the time that is gone. It's past and it will never return. How then can I redeem time? What does redemption mean in the New Testament? Redemption is what Jesus Christ went to the cross to do. To redeem people we say, to save souls from hell, from the judgment of sin. And when a man has come to know Jesus Christ as his personal Savior, we say that he is redeemed. How can I redeem my time? By letting my time be redeemed from sin that it might be used for the glory of God instead of the satisfaction of self, that it might be used for my Lord and to produce for my Lord instead of for fleshly lust and for lustful satisfactions. Yes, we are accountable for our time, not for just a fraction of it, but all of it. God does not ask for just a seventh of your time, he asks for all of your time. But he prescribes a way in which part of it will be used as a testimony of your stewardship, a testimony of his sovereignty over the days and the months and the years that you may be given. Some of us may be given five talents worth of time and some of us may be given only two talents worth of time, and some of us may be given only one talent worth of time, some will live longer than others. It is not a question of how long you live. It's how you live for the glory of God.

Our material possessions are the same. These are things that are given to us of God. God is not asking that we use a fraction of them. If these things represent the hours, the sweat, and the energy of your life to produce and to get and to gather these things, then the way in which you use them is the way in which you are using your life. You are living for that which you spend your money for. Don't fracture your life. Don't split your personality. Don't be a spiritual schizophrenic by failing to be fully dedicated to God.

God is the owner of all things, not a fraction of the world, but all of it. You and I are stewards of the whole life, not a fraction of it, but all of it. Then when we say with Frances Havergal, "Take my life and let it be consecrated Lord to thee," we are saying, "Lord take all my life, not a fraction of it."

5.
Life: Profit or Loss

"Life, profit or loss?" These are business terms and life is one of the most serious businesses you can be involved in. It's a lifetime concern to most of us, if not all of us, as to whether we really profit from life or whether it is a total loss. We need to have a philosophy of life. We are thinking in terms of the total life, the whole life, and what it is we are living for.

What Is Life?

To some people life is what it gets and this becomes their life—the process of getting. We start out in life wanting to get ahead. In fact, most of us want to get a head start above and before everybody else. The young people may not have thought about it yet, but most of the adults have, that the younger generation seem to be wanting to take off from where their parents are. Most young couples getting married today want a house, not an apartment; they want two automobiles and the same standard of living that they have been accustomed to. They are wanting to take on where the parents are after maybe twenty-five years of marriage and building their life. From this point the younger generation want to launch on to bigger and better things instead of being willing to start, each one, at a reasonable starting place. A lot of our problems today are related to this problem of trying to adjust ourselves to a standard of living. The problem at the root of it all is that we haven't really decided what life is for. Is life merely for getting? There is an old saying: "Get what you can get while the getting's good and can what you can while the canning's good." This seems to be the philosophy of a lot of people. The Word of God has some things to say about this kind of philosophy.

Paul for example says to Timothy, "the love of money is the root of all evil." (1 Tim. 6:10) Now notice he did not say that *money* is the root of all evil. Money is amoral. It is neither moral nor immoral. We are using the word money in a general sense, not necessarily talking about coins or currency, but money as it represents material possessions. All of our material possessions are amoral. That is, their morality is determined by the user. Money becomes immoral when it is used for immoral purposes. The same dollar that could be a man's tithe as he came to worship could well have been the dollar that was put in the hand of Judas by the priest buying him to betray Jesus. The same dollar! What's the difference? The difference was in the use. One man could worship God with it, the next man can cause murder with it. This is not the problem or the fault of the money. The problem or the fault is found in the heart of the man that possesses it, because he says "the *love* of money is the root of all evil" and love is a passion of the human heart. It is an attachment, an affection that becomes a motivation and in this motivation of material things, in this passion for getting things, is really the root of evil in our world today. You can look at the Ten Commandments and realize that the love of money, has caused man to break every one of them. Men have committed murder for money, they have committed adultery for money, they've broken the sabbath for money, they've denied and destroyed their parents for money, and you can go right on through the list, every one of them, can be broken for the love of money.

Or we can go to another verse and find when Paul wrote to the Colossians, he said, "Covetousness is idolatry" (Col. 3:5). Now here in America we are accustomed to thinking of Christianity as our religion, not because America is Christian as such, but because Christianity is the predominant religion in our country. It involves the affiliation of more people than any other religion or all the other religions put together in America. So we don't think of ourselves as being an idolatrous nation. We are repulsed at the thought that America would be guilty of idolatry. But stop and listen to what he said, "Covetousness is idolatry." You do not have to have the statutes of pagan gods on the mantel of your home to be guilty of idolatry. Anything, and I would underscore that word anything, anything that comes to be of primary importance to you and of more influence in your life than God himself, that thing has become your god. Covetousness, that desire for something that somebody else has. The old race that we've talked about and joked about through the years, of keeping up with the Joneses, really it isn't a joke anymore. In fact it has been said that in this day and age that the problem in trying to keep up with the Joneses is that when you think you've about caught up with them, they've refinanced. But this business of just trying to keep up with our neighbors is in itself in danger of being covetousness in its real nature. Covetousness, a driving desire to gather things, just for the sake of gathering things, Paul said, is idolatry. Now then if life consists of what it gets, what it produces, then my success in life is measured by what I have been able to get and to keep. My monetary value, my assets become the measure of my success and this becomes the driving passion of my life. This is covetousness, this is idolatry, and I challenge you to give that a few hours reflection and see if America is not guilty of idolatry.

Just always trying to get is selfishness and materialism and we loose sight of the real values in life. When you boil life down to this, you find yourself in confrontation with the words of our Lord when he said, "A man's life consisteth not in the abundance of the things which he possesseth" (Luke 12:15). Then life is not getting. Life is giving.

This is the second philosophy: "life is giving." Some years ago

I read the story of a man who had been quite wealthy until the time of the great depression in our country. Just prior to the economic collapse he had given a large sum of money to a college to build a building. And then the depression came and he lost everything he had. One day in the depth of the depression, he walked onto the college campus and looked at the building that he had built with the last of his wealth before his complete economic collapse. As he stood there just looking at that building, someone recognized him and recognized also that this man had lost his total wealth after giving that building to the school. He asked him, "Sir, do you have any regrets for having given that large amount of money for this building? Would you rather not have kept it realizing that you have lost everything else?" And without a moment's hesitation, he said, "no sir, I have no regrets. That building I gave is all I have. If I had kept it, I would have lost it too." This can give us some serious reflection to realize that really what we have spent we have had, but what we give away we have because we have the joy of it. It's like the rose. The fragrance of the rose which we can all enjoy is found only in its giving. A flower that retains its fragrance for itself really has no fragrance, at least not for the enjoyment of mankind. Only in its giving is it enjoyed. And this is true for us, for life. Life that would have a fragrance to be enjoyed by those around us must be an outgoing, a giving life.

We need to find a philosophy of life then that identifies us with the outgo, not just the income; that we can find a real sound basis for living. There is a verse of Scripture that was brought to my attention some years ago in the course of Bible study which has said a lot to me. It's found in Ephesians the fourth chapter, the twenty-eighth verse, when Paul said, "Let him that stole steal no more; but rather let him labour, working with his hands the thing which is good, that he may have to give to him that needeth." Why do we labor, why do we work? Are we working in order to get? Is payday the ultimate? Is this the real goal in our lives as we get up in the morning and go to work? Is this our motivation? In order to earn and to get? Paul said our motivation for labor should be "in order to be able to give." In order to be able to give! We can only give that which we have, we cannot give that which we do not have. So there is a two-fold process in preparation to giving. There is the earning and the getting. There is the labor that goes into it and then the receiving of the fruit of labor. And in those two steps we prepare for the greatest step of life, that of giving. Paul said this should be our motive. If you will reflect on it again, I believe that Paul is identifying theft itself with the materialistic motive of getting. Always trying to get. That's what makes a man a thief. He's doing the same thing the honest laborer is doing, he's getting, but he's laid aside the honesty in the process. But at heart his motivation may be the same. Both of them just trying to get something they don't have, one of them fearless enough to defy the law in doing so. But down underneath the materialistic motive is the driving force for them both and for neither of them should this motive be sufficient. For a Christian the motive of getting is not enough, he needs to have that Christian motive to give. This should be life. When the gift of God's love has come into our own hearts we in turn will respond in a spirit of giving. This is when we really find the Christian principle of life.

Standards of Profit and Loss

Now back to our first question of profit or loss. You have to define your terms before you can measure your success. You have to know your objective or you will never know when you have arrived. You must identify the milestones or you cannot measure your progress. And if you are going to talk about profit and loss in life, you are going to have to know what your measurement is. Is it purely monetary? Or is there another?

As I have studied, thought, and prayed about this subject for some time, number of years, in fact, I have come to the conclusion that we live largely at least for that for which we spend our money.

Do you realize that we spend more of our time in that pursuit which is identified by a paycheck than we do in any other one thing? Then that paycheck represents more of life's time and energy than does any other one thing. And when you spend a paycheck, you are spending that many hours of your life and all the energy and strength and opportunity of mind, body, and soul that went into it. That's what you are spending your life for. We ought to think about that when we set down for ourselves a pay plan which they call "easy payments." How many paychecks and hours that add up to weeks in your life do you want to spend in this? That's what you are spending your life for. Now this doesn't mean to say that material things are evil or that we ought not to possess them. I'm simply saying that when we start to identify the profit or the loss of life, we are going to have to establish our goals. What are we living for? If we are living only for the paycheck, then the ultimate of it is that we are living for what we spend the paycheck for. That identifies an awful lot of our lives.

We can live for material things or spiritual things. We can use our money in a way that it will gather to us other material things. We can barter in the marketplace with it, or we can use it in such a way that it will bring spiritual blessings into our lives. Would you rather be wealthy or happy? You can't measure happiness with money. You can't buy happiness for money. You can buy a bed, but you can't buy a night's sleep. You can buy food or you can buy medicine, but you can't buy health. And many a man has found out that there is a vast difference between wealth and health or happiness.

There was a very successful physician in my hometown. He was our family doctor for many years. He told my father on one occasion, "You can tell your people that wealth does not buy happiness." He said, "I have enough wealth that my children and their children could live on the same standard of living as they have been accustomed to living on without working another day in their lives, but you can tell your people for me that it doesn't bring happiness."

There is a difference between the material and the spiritual. Where are your goals? These goals are going to determine the profit or the loss of your life—whether you are gaining or losing, whether you are getting out of life what you want or not. Paul also tells us that the things that are visible are temporal, that is, they last awhile and then they pass away. Whereas the invisible, he says, is eternal. (2 Cor. 4:18). Invisible things are things such as love and truth, happiness, joy, the same kind of things that Paul identified as being the fruits of the Spirit (Gal. 5:22–23). These are the invisible things. You can't see love, but you can experience it. Which do you want in life? Are you going to prove a profit or a loss of your life? Is it successful? Jesus asked the question, "What profiteth a man if he gains the whole world and loses his own soul?" What's the profit of life if a man's total being is found in material things and his total loss is in the spiritual column? There comes a time when you can't take it with you, you know.

Some years ago I made that statement in a small group and a lady spoke up and said, "If I can't take it with me, I'm not going." And I said, "Lady, there are no pockets in shrouds." She said, "there will be in mine because I'm going to sew them in." But she didn't. I don't know whether she got busy and forgot it, but when she left she didn't take it with her. Someone asked about a man who died, "How much did he leave?" And a friend who seemed to understand him well replied, "He didn't leave anything, God took him away from all of it." But somehow there will be a parting of a man from his possessions and that's the reason that we dare not make it our lives.

We must somehow identify our lives with the spiritual and with the eternal for a man's soul ought not to be identified with the material and temporal things that shall pass away, for that soul of his, created in the image of God, is eternal. Have you chosen the goals in life? Have you found out how to determine whether your life is winning or losing, a profit or loss?

In this day and age, we hear a lot about poverty and war on

poverty, trying to determine where is the line of poverty above which you have a standard of living that's acceptable and below which you are substandard. Where is that line? Where is the line that we draw below which we say a man is poor?" I read a good definition of this the other day. Someone said, "the poor man is the man who has much to live on and nothing to live for." Perhaps this will help us somehow to get our values right and find out what really counts in life so that we will know whether life is a profit or a loss, whether we're winning or losing, whether life ultimately will be a success.

6.
Three Reasons Why

One of the common questions of childhood is "why?" And it is not a bad question. From time to time those of us who think of ourselves as adults could well confront ourselves with the question "why?" On one occasion when the followers of Christ were numerous, they hastened around the edge of the sea of Galilee in order to meet him on the other side. He questioned their motives. He said they were following him not because they were concerned about his mission, or eternal life, but because he had fed them bread the day before. That was the "why." In other words he was saying they were following him because of what they could get out of it for themselves. They were not looking for a leader to lead them into greater things, they were not looking for open doors to greater service, they were not looking for opportunities to achieve higher ground and to become more closely identified with God or to become a close intimate follower with his son, Jesus Christ. These, he was saying, were not their motives. Their "why" was purely the hunger of the body because he had fed them bread. Sometimes when we have reason to talk with people about their involvement in the work of the Lord, we hear a why. Perhaps we talk to someone about his relationship to the Lord and to the Lord's Day and why he should set aside one day out of seven. Sometimes we see those who have given so much more of themselves and of their time than just one day; people who give hours of time for committee service or organizational leadership. Occasionally someone says "why?" It isn't always because they have time on their hands. Sometimes the people who are doing the most are the busiest. I mean they are the busiest without these involvements.

Sometimes we see those who are so openly and obviously committed to God and to his church in the giving of his tithe and someone says "why?" Or we learn of someone else who has gone beyond the tithe to 11 percent or 12 percent or some to 20 percent. One Christian man had a reputation of giving 90 percent of his wealth. He was a man who had risen from bankruptcy to become a millionaire and gave God the glory for it. And all the time that he was increasing in his income, he was increasing also in his outgo, for the word of God. Why? What is the motivation for this kind of thing? As I said, it is a good question and it ought to be answered. If you are among those who are giving much of your time to the work of Christ and to service in your church, you might be wondering why some days. When you are tired, you are wondering, well, why should I do it? Or maybe you are anticipating an approach from the nominating committee or an organizational leader in the next few weeks and you are saying to yourself, why should I do this? Or you may feel compelled to ask the one who contacts you, "why should I take that position of service?" Or perhaps you who are confronted with the fact that you are not giving of your time to the work of God and to your church and you feel just a cringe of guilt from time to time. You feel a sense of really not doing what you know is your part and you are saying, well, why should I? Or perhaps you have been confronted recently with the challenge to become a tither of your income, and again you are saying, well, why?

For all of these questions and all of these involvements of our time, our talents, our tithes, and our offerings, there are at least three good reasons why Christians should respond to the love of God in such a way as this.

The Law and Duty—the Bible

The first one is because of law and duty. This one is usually expressed in words related to the Bible. You say, "Well, the Bible teaches it." We frequently hear people say that you ought to be a tither because it is in the Bible or you ought to be a worker in the church because its scriptural. Then we can take the Bible and show that every Christian ought to be a soul-winner just as easily as we can say that every church member ought to be a tither. In all of these involvements, we begin by saying, "the Bible says." When I say it is a matter of law, it is not necessarily that I am referring to the Ten Commandments nor to the Old Testament. There are laws and commandments in the New Testament also. But what I am saying is, here is an elementary experience. Paul in talking about the law as related to his personal life, said, "the law was like a schoolteacher that brought me to Jesus." It's an elementary thing. It's the one that begins to teach us to read. It's the one that teaches us of our relationships to other people. You see the child, the infant, has no awareness of personalities. Then there comes that stage of development when a child becomes aware of himself and he begins to use the pronoun "mine" or "me." He may not even use it properly so far as the English language is concerned, but he is beginning to express a knowledge of the fact that "I am here." This may be a matter of selfishness. This toy "belongs to me," and he will cry and say "mine" if somebody else reaches for it. But it is an evidence of a self-awareness and it is the beginning of this development of the child that the teacher has to lead him to be aware of others and to learn to share with others. It is a matter of teaching and of training and there are teachings of this nature in the law.

Now, when Paul referred to the law, obviously he was referring to the Old Testament because the New Testament had not been written. He was in the process of writing part of it. But he was saying that the law teaches us concerning sin. The law tells me that

I am a sinner because it shows me what I ought to do and what I'm not doing. It also tells me things that I ought not to do that I'm still doing. The law teaches me that I'm a sinner and that I'm not doing right. And it is through the teachings and principles of the law, he said, that I came to know the Savior. He came to realize his need for a Savior. Well, it is this kind of elementary thing that we can speak of also in our Christian experience and development. The first appeal that we make to a new Christian is to say to him, "The Bible teaches you that you should do thus and so." This is not a wrong motive, it is a good one. It's an elementary one, but it is a good one because a Christian along with many other things that he learns and believes, begins usually with reading the Bible and he comes to a place of faith to say, "I believe the Bible, I believe it is the Word of God." He may not understand it, he may not be able to explain its inspiration. There may be some passages of Scripture, that he will not understand as a new Christian, but yet he will say he believes the Bible. He will understand it more later but he believes it now. He has confidence in the Book and so his Sunday School teacher, his pastor, his Christian friend, a member of his family perhaps, will be able to take a verse of the Scripture or a chapter of Scripture and say what is expected of him. Now notice that "say what's expected of him." In other words, here by the teachings of the plain written Word of God, we begin to develop a sense of duty, a sense of obligation, a sense of responsibility that is founded on the simple statement, "It's in the Bible."

When a man says, concerning tithing for example, that it's a matter of law, it sure is. But don't say that it is "just" a matter of law. It depends a little on your definition of law. If you are talking about the law in the sense of the Mosaic law, yes it's that. But if you think that's the beginning of it, you really haven't read the Bible, have you? You haven't done your homework, because we find that virtually all of the things that were in there were already being practiced. When God said in that tablet of stone, "Thou shalt not kill," do you mean to tell me that's the first time those people found out that a human life was precious and ought not to be taken by the hand of another? When God said, "Thou shalt not commit adultery," do you mean to tell me that those family units that were gathered together there in the camp of Israel at the foot of Mt. Sinai had never heard of the sanctity of marriage before? Of course not! We go back to the beginning and find that God began with one man and one woman and expected them to be loyal to each other although he had never written it down for them. Somehow, they were so created in the image of God that they were given a capability to understand and to grasp that love was a mutual thing and it's a pure thing and it demands something of us. They didn't have to have a book written or a picture drawn in order to show it to them.

Now then concerning the matter of tithing, we find that Abraham practiced tithing four hundred years before Moses brought the law down from Mt. Sinai. If you say that tithing is a matter of law, well, yes it is. It's a matter of the revealed will of God. It's a matter of a part of God's plan for his universe. You'd have to revise and change this universe if you were going to do something with the seven-day-a-week cycle. God made the world that way. And God made the world of things and the world of people in such a way that he retained a relationship to both man and things. And that relationship of man and things and God is expressed in one day a week of worship and one tenth of a man's income. That's law, not because Moses brought it down on a tablet of stone, but because God wrote it in the tablets of human hearts. We have a responsibility to God. When Adam was given the assignment of taking care of the garden, God didn't write it down in a book, but Adam understand that the garden belonged to God and he was just the gardener, that's all. So really it was no new revelation when God wrote things like that into the Mosaic law, it had been in practice for hundreds and hundreds of years. Yes, it is a matter of law, it is a matter of duty, it is a matter of obligation, it's a matter of responsibility. It's a matter of a basic primary relationship to God. And when we learn this, whether we learn it by reading it from a page or whether we learn it by the teaching of a teacher or an example of a Christian friend, or by the instruction of a family member, it is still a part of the elementary development of an individual to know "this I ought to do."

We find it in Malachi 3:10 spoken very plainly, but in the context in which the people of God had forsaken it. God was bringing them back to what they had known for centuries. Now, in the days of our Lord, they were practicing it. They were tithing the little things of the garden even—like pulling the carrots and the radishes and spreading them out and counting them very meticulously and giving one out of every ten to the priest. This they could do. But they had forgotten how to practice justice and mercy and to demonstrate faith. Jesus criticized them for their lack of justice and their lack of mercy, but he did not criticize them for tithing. He was simply pointing out to them, you have done some of the elementary, outer things, but your heart still is not right. You see you are not going to go to heaven because you tithe. But that doesn't change the fact that it's there. Jesus did not set aside the law. He didn't say now that I have come to reveal the fulness of the grace of God, you no longer have to be honest, you no longer have to abstain from murder, you no longer have to abstain from adultery.

Now that's what the new morality would say to you: "We're above their law. We don't have to live by these old-fashioned laws." God has written it into the nature of his universe and into the nature of man made in the image of God that a man shall respect the wife and the possessions of another. That's the reason that murder is out and that adultery is out and these other things that hurt people are out. Not because they are written on a tablet of stone or printed out in a book of paper, but because God has implanted it in the nature of his universe; and when you violate that, it's a violation of the law of God, even if you never read it in the Book. Now then Jesus did not set these things aside. He did not change the cycle of the days of the week, he did not set aside man's need to worship nor did he set aside the teaching of God's Word that a man ought not to come into the presence of God without a gift. Man comes to worship God bringing himself and bringing of his possessions as an expression of thanksgiving and gratitude to God. The law teaches us all of these things. And because I've read it, because I've been taught it and because I've learned it, I want to do it. And so many Christians, when asked why they are so faithful and loyal to the worship services of their church answer, "Well, because my Bible teaches me that Christians are expected to worship, that's why." Or you ask one, "Why do you tithe?" and he says, "Because the Bible teaches it." He's right. That's one reason, that's one motive for doing it, but it is not the only motive.

Loyalty and Dedication—the Church

You'll get a different answer from some people. You will find that not only is it a matter of law and duty because they read it in the Book, but you will find that for some it's a matter of loyalty and devotion to their church, to the church, not as an institution and certainly not as a building, but as a fellowship of people that have come to know, have come to love, and have had a common experience with Jesus Christ. This has drawn us together around the Christ of the cross and of the empty tomb. He is our Savior, our Lord, and we have him in common. And because of loyalty and devotion to this fellowship, I do these things. I participate in the things the church is doing because I am a part of it and really the church cannot do it as it ought to do it unless I am a part of it because I'm part of the body and therefore I must be a part of the doing. So out of loyalty to the fellowship I do these things, out of devotion to the church for what it has done for me. Using the word "church" in the continuing or as some would say, the generic sense, because in my life I have been associated with many churches, many local fellowships of believers, but across the years of my life, the church, (the churches of which I have been privileged to be a part) have made great investments in my life.

It was a church that helped to teach me the things I ought to know as a boy. It was in a church that I made a public profession of faith and was baptized, and I cherish that experience. It was because of a church that I had that experience. Oh, I know a Christian home and a preacher daddy contributed to it, of course. But I also am aware of the fact that although my father was a preacher, he was not my pastor until I graduated from high school, because he was preaching in different places and I was going to church in one place where we lived. That church had a continuing influence in my life. My first experience of public speaking was in a church. My first opportunity to stand and speak a word for my Lord was because of a church. It was through the investments of churches that provided a college for my education and a seminary for my education. It was through an association in a church school that I met my wife. It was by the graces of a good many Baptist churches through their cooperative mission program that part of my education was paid for. I didn't pay for it. They did. I have a debt of obligation. I have a debt of loyalty and devotion to churches that have had a part in these things in my life. Just out of loyalty to the church for what it stands for, for what it has done for me, and for what I can do for others through my church, out of this kind of loyalty and devotion, I want to do these things. I want to strengthen my church by adding my prayers to those of the brethren. I want to strengthen my church by being present when my church worships. I want to strengthen my church by participating when my church goes visiting, when my church goes out knocking on doors to find people without Christ, without God, without a church, without hope perhaps. I want to be a part of that because my church is doing that. Out of loyalty and devotion to my church and what it stands for, I want to be a part of whatever it is doing.

Therefore, I not only give of my time and my talents, but I want to give of my material possessions. You'll hear an answer like this from some when you ask them, "why?" I can tell you why. It's not just because it is in the Bible. It's because my heart and life are locked up in the fellowship of this church and what it is as well as what it does. Consequently, when I see the value of what my church is doing, when I see the ministry it is performing for people in our own community, when I see and evaluate something of its outreach and the spreading of the gospel and sending of missionaries to far parts of the world, I want to have a part of these things. I don't want to be a short-sighted provincial sort of person who has no concern for towns on down the road. I don't want to be that kind of a narrow person that has no understanding of human needs in other countries of the world. I want to share in some way to meet human need wherever it is. And I know that the greatest need that man has is for God. His greatest need is spiritual. I want to have a part in feeding the hungry, clothing the naked, housing those that have no homes. But I don't just want to do these things and leave that man without God. A man well dressed is hopeless without Christ. A man well fed is hopeless without Christ. A man living in a beautiful home is hopeless without Christ. I not only want to clothe and feed his body and cover his head, I want to give hope to his heart. Therefore I want a part in sharing the gospel of Christ with these people wherever they are, whether they are down and out or up and out, whether they are here or there. My church has a plan for this sort of thing and I am a part of this plan because I am a part of my church.

You will find some will say to you: "Why do I give my time? Because my church cannot do anything except as it is done through the hands and the feet and the money of those that are the church." That's it! How much would your church be doing today if it were totally dependent upon people like you to do just what you are now doing. If every member of the church gave no more time to the work of the Lord than you do, how much work would your church accomplish? If nobody allowed their talents to be used anymore frequently, anymore thoroughly, anymore dedicatedly than you do yours, how many souls would we have, how many teachers would we have, how many door-to-door visits would we have? If nobody gave any more of their material possessions to support the work of the church than you give, how much would we be able to do? I'm afraid probably the first thing we would have to do if none of them gave any more than some give, we would have to turn the air-conditioning off. The television broadcast would have to go off. We would have to cancel the insurance on the buildings, and we would have to call off our commitments for mission buildings and missionaries here in our own town as well as around the world. These are serious things we are talking about. So somebody says, "The reason I'm a tither, the reason I'm a soul-winner, the reason that I'm a worker in my church is because of loyalty and devotion to my church for what it is and for what it does and I want a part in it."

I think a verse from Paul's letter to Timothy has an application here. He said, "The man who does not provide for his own, especially for those of his own household, has denied the faith and is worse than an infidel." Strong language. Especially when he said "those of his own household." He's talking about the man who is supposed to provide for his children and his wife and who claims to be a Christian and does not provide for his family is something less than a Christian in that regard. Now if there are circumstances beyond his control that leave him incapable of employment or something of that sort, then his Christian brother will help him. But the man who is too lazy, too slovenly to provide for his own family is a disgrace to the name of Christians, Paul is saying. In the first part of that verse, he said, "He that provides not for his own." He then went on to say, "especially for those of his own house." But who is included in "his own" that are not included in "his house"? Could it include his own church? Could it include his friends? Could it include those programs, plans, performances in which he is involved because he has identified himself with some things that some other people are doing? If he is a member of a civic club, you can depend on two things: he is attending the meetings and paying the dues. But he can be a member of a church and do neither. That is using the term loosely—he can be a member.

He can have his name on the roll so that it will show up in a newspaper when his obituary is printed, but so far as the ways and the work of the Lord through that church is concerned, is he really a member? If he is not supporting the body? If he is not walking when the body walks? If he is not working with his hands when the body works with its hands? If his voice is never raised in the cause of Christ when the church is supposed to be speaking? Is he really a part? What is his part? If when the church takes upon itself an obligation and a responsibility to project itself and its gospel out beyond its four walls, is there one identified with that body that says, "I have no part in this?" Why?

This reminds me of a story, an old story, of a church that was taking a missionary offering. As they passed the plate by one man refused to put anything in. He said, "I don't believe in missions." The man who passed the plate was a real quick thinker and he just passed the plate right back to him and said, "Well, take some out then. It's for the heathen." You see you are either in or you're out. You are either a force or a field. You are either a missionary or you are one to be sought by the missionary. You are either a part of what is going on or you are the object of it. You can take your choice. That's really what Paul was saying, I think, when he said, "A man that does not provide for his own, especially those of his own house, has denied the faith." The man that doesn't share in the ministries and the responsibilities of his church with his time, his talents, and his treasure is denying that he believed. Because he said when he joined that he believed in these things, but if he is not becoming a part of the doing of these things, then he is denying that he believes these things. It's just as simple as that. We need to recognize that there is a motivation, a justifiable motivation of loyalty. There are some things that I do for my church because I am a member of it that I might not have done for any other reason. For just the fact that my church is doing it, I want to be a part of it. And that's a good motive. But there is another motive that can be given.

Love and Devotion—the Lord

There's another reason that some will give you when you ask, "Why do you do these things?" They will not tell you, "Because it is in the Bible," and they'll not tell you because "I want to be loyal to my church." Both of these have a sense of duty, a sense of obligation to them. They are good motives, you understand. They are not wrong. But there's a higher one and that's love and dedication to the Lord.

Paul expressed it when he wrote to the Colossians. He told them that whatever they did, whether they were eating or drinking or whatever they did, they should do it as unto the Lord (Col. 3:17, 23). There are some things that the law may not require, and there are those that would argue this and say: "I don't *have* to tithe. The law doesn't demand that I do it." I think you are wrong, in fact, in my heart, I know you are wrong. But even if you were right, if you could prove to me from the Bible that I didn't have to tithe, I'd still do it and I will tell you why. Yes, I want to be loyal to my church, but I love my Lord. And if it would be unlawful for a Jew to give less than a tithe, it surely would be disgraceful for a Christian to give less than a tithe. That's the conviction of my own heart. That's what I've learned about my own Lord. "After all he's done for me, how can I do less than give him my best and live for him completely?" Just plain simple old-fashioned love. There are some things some men would do for their wives, without having to review the marriage vows to see whether or not they committed themselves to it. But just in the growing experience of fellowship together through the years, they have fallen deeper and deeper in love and they try increasingly to do more and more for each other, just because of love. Not because the law of the land is going to call them adulterers if they don't do these things, not because the vows of their wedding day are going to make them look pretty low if they don't do these things. They are not concerned about what the law requires. They are not concerned about the vows expressed. They are concerned only about the fact that they're in love, and there is no higher motive than this.

That's the motive that took Jesus to Calvary. He didn't go because the law required it. He didn't go out of loyalty to that little band of tearful people standing at the foot of the cross who had forsaken him a few hours before. He went to the cross because he loved us. That's why many Christians are faithful in the attendance of the worship services of our church. That's the reason that many of them are faithful to participate in the work of their church. That's the reason many of them are faithful in tithing and in giving offerings in support of their church—because they see that the church is "the body of Christ."

Paul before his conversion, "played havoc with the church," the Scriptures say. History records that he persecuted the church and on the day of his conversion Jesus said to him, "Saul, Saul, why persecuteth thou me?" I remind you that what you do to the church you do to Christ. If you don't love the church, you don't love Christ. If you don't give of yourself to the church, you are not giving of yourself to Christ. If you ignore and despise the church, you are ignoring and despising Christ. If you don't share of your material blessings with the church, you are not sharing of your material blessings with Christ. There is no organization or institution in this world except the church and the home that have been organized, instituted, and blessed of God. And the church is said to be "the body of Christ." Because I love him, I'll support the body. Because I love him, I'll be loyal and faithful to the body. Because I love him, I'll give myself to him through my church. That's why. Why do you do what you do?

7.
Churches Are Stewards, Too

There are some questions that are asked by most churches, if not all churches in relationship to their stewardship. One is "how to budge the budget"; the second is "how to take the stew out of stewardship"; and the third is "how to remove the pain from campaign." Now, if you could answer those three questions for most churches, they would be satisfied. Well, really, to answer all three of those questions, what you need to do is to "discipline the disciples" and put "Christ into your Christianity." Now, that will answer most of the questions if not all of them, but we need to look for some practical things, some things that are immediately applicable to my situation. That is what practical means to me. It doesn't mean that it isn't practical to be spiritual. It means that when I can take the Scriptures and make them immediately applicable to my present situation, then it is practical because it then becomes practiceable.

Points From Paul

Paul points out that the task they were about to do which related directly and immediately to the offering that they were taking for the poor saints in Jerusalem was a responsibility of *all* the churches. Churches are responsible for many things. We know that they are responsible for evangelism. They are responsible for missions. They are responsible for Christian actions of many sorts to meet human needs. This is the business of the church, to meet human needs wherever they are found in the name of Christ that he may have the glory. Paul pointed out to this church that he was not asking anything of them that he was not asking of all the others. It was a responsibility of all the churches. He said, as we read in 1 Corinthians 16:1, "As I have told all the churches of Galatia, so do ye." So from that verse and other references, we know that he had the same approach to the churches of Galatia and the churches of Macedonia and now in these epistles to the church in Corinth. It was a responsibility of all the churches. That was the first point, from Paul.

The second point from Paul was that it was to be an equal responsibility. How can you find equality between churches? Well, it is difficult for anybody to sit down and figure out a formula. But there is a basis on which there can be equality. For example, when we think in terms of money for missionary causes and we want all of the churches to participate. There is a difference of economic circumstance between churches just as there is between individuals. Upon what basis can we call for equality?

Well, the simplest answer and the one most commonly used is to put it on a percentage basis so that each church can give a percentage of its budget. That's about the only reasonable way to do it and yet that is not necessarily equality because the circumstances are not always the same. When you are talking about the budget, you are talking about the velocity of the flow of resources through that church. But there are many churches just as there are many individuals who are not reaching their potential and to say that a church is doing its share because it is giving a reasonable percentage of that which is going through its treasury is not necessarily true. It may be that the church, meaning the people of that congregation, are not doing what they ought to do toward their own church in the first place. Whereas some other church that may have less money, actually may be giving the widow's mite. They may be giving closer to their actual potential than some other church which has perhaps more money in dollars and cents. But when you are talking about equality, you are not talking about dollars and cents, you are talking about ability. You have to come back to what Paul said here, he not only mentions the matter of equality in these verses but he says in another verse that "if there were a willing mind, it was accepted according to that which a man has, not that which he has not." So it is accepted on the basis of one's ability. But not only that, for he says in the next chapter: "Every man as he purposeth in his heart so let him give. Not grudgingly or of necessity for God loveth a cheerful giver." When we start talking about equality, you have to talk about ability in terms of actual possessions, dollars and cents, if its money you are talking about. At the same time, you have to put into it that spiritual equality of the willingness of the people, as well as their actual and potential abilities. These are things that are involved in equality. We don't tell the individual how much he has to give, either. We can preach to him the principles and we can teach him the doctrines, but when it comes right down to writing the check, he is going to do as he pleases. And that is the way it ought to be. That's the only way it can be. We have to wait for the individual to be moved by the Spirit of God so that he will love and will want to give. The church as a body has to be moved in similar fashion and so this really is all involved in this matter of equality.

Another point here is the responsibility of the churches to decide who will handle its funds. Paul was going from church to church and those that were working with Paul, his fellow laborers, some of them were going with him and some were going to other churches and they were getting the offering and getting it together and were going to take it in one trip to Jerusalem. These people that were helping to gather the funds from the churches as the churches had gathered them in the church. In verse 19 he says, these people were "chosen by the churches to travel with us" in regard to this offering. The church had a responsibility, for the designation, the delegation, the election, if you please, of responsible leadership. Paul points out that these needed to be trustworthy people, people who had the confidence of the churches, people who would handle the affairs in an honest manner. But the responsibility rested with the churches to determine who would handle their funds. It wasn't the responsibility of the preacher, but the church.

I notice also that it was the responsibility of the churches to see to it that the funds were, as he says here, administered in a way that would be honest in all ways before the Lord and before men. The administration of these funds was a responsibility of the church. And then underline the whole thing once again. You just can't talk about material things even in a Christian context without getting back to the fundamental of love. "God so loved that he gave." And he expects those of us who know his love to be giving, giving of ourselves, giving of our time, our talents, as well as our treasures. In the last verse of the eighth chapter he says, "Wherefore show ye to them, and before the churches, the proof of your love, and of our boasting on your behalf." Paul had evidently boasted to the churches of Macedonia of what the church in Corinth had promised to do. That's the reason he wrote these letters to them, the second letter particularly, because they had made a promise of what they were going to do and the committee was already on its way to get the money. He didn't want them not to have it, and that's the reason he wrote and told them to "lay it aside on the first day of the week," week by week, so that we won't be embarrassed when they come to get the money, and you will fulfil the pledge that you made.

In the same chapter we read: "now therefore perform the doing of it. That as there was a readiness to will, so there may be a performance also out of that which ye have." We need to make pledges, but we need also to have performances. These are some points from Paul.

Churches Are Stewards, Too

Churches are stewards, too. In the first place, the church is a steward of the Word of God. We have the responsibility of getting the Word of Jesus Christ out to the world. I read an interesting story recently. It's an old story, it happened near forty years ago. In 1930 radio was in its infancy and the King of England was supposed to make a historic speech that was to be carried to the entire commonwealth by radio. It was one of the first times, if not the first time, that such a thing had happened, and of course there was a great deal of tension about it. After all, the king was going to speak. King George was scheduled for a set hour when he would step to the microphone and speak to his people. A man from the radio network, since radio was new, had homework to do. He had done a lot of studying about what makes radio operate and how does it operate and what do you do. He had anticipated every problem that he could think of so that if an emergency arose when the king was speaking he would know what to do about it. Well, one came up that he hadn't anticipated. Just seconds before the king was to speak his first words, the man from the network discovered a broken wire in the broadcasting equipment and there was not time to fix it before the king was to speak. So he took those two wires in his two hands and for fifteen minutes King George of England spoke through the body of the man. He let his body be the channel of that current that was going through the radio station for fifteen minutes because he said, "The speech of the king must go out." Somehow or other, I believe we must get a spirit of commitment like this: We must recognize the message of the King, the gospel of the Christ, must go out. We have it in our hands. It's not ours, it's his.

Therefore we are stewards of the Word of God, we are caretakers of it. He didn't give it to us to put it under a glass in a museum someplace to say "this is a Bible." He's giving it to us that we might proclaim it to the world. We are stewards of the message of Jesus

Christ. This must make everyone of us a witness for Christ. This must make us all soul-winners for Christ. In a sense we must all be preachers of the gospel. It is the responsibility of the church as we find in the New Testament, to get the message out. This involves the training of the workers. This involves the sending of the missionaries. We find in the Scriptures that the church was the one that sent them out, and this is the way that God wants it done today. We are stewards of the Word.

That brings us to a second thing of which we are stewards. We are stewards of people. Many churches do not realize this, I fear. But we are stewards of people. The Bible says, for example in Acts, "the Lord added unto the church daily those who were being saved." He added them to the church. The greatest resource the church has is its people, not its bank account. Paul tells the church in Ephesus that God had given people like evangelists and teachers and pastors to the churches for the equipping of the saints for the work of the ministry. This is somehow the work of the church, to train its people and to prepare its people.

But that is not all either. One of the tasks of the church as a body is to see to it that it has a program, a plan of work that is big enough to challenge the best in every one of us. I'm afraid we plan too small. We think too little. And our plans are not big enough for ourselves, must less for God.

In one of my first pastorates I was attempting to get a little country church to adopt a budget. In the history of the church they had never had a budget. The treasurer brought the bills to the business meeting each month and they voted which ones they were going to pay. I was trying to lead them into having a budget and to having missions in the budget on a percentage basis. In a business meeting one of the men stood up to encourage the congregation to do something about it. Just a few months before that little church had voted to have preaching twice a month instead of once a month. He made reference to that historic decision when he said, "We can do this thing that our pastor is asking us to do, if we want to." He said, "when our church voted to go from quarter-time to half-time," (that means to go to preaching twice a month instead of once), "I increased my tithe from twenty-five to thirty-five cents a week, and I can do it again if I have to." I thought, brother you sure could and without missing it! For a long time I was very critical of him. I thought, That successful farmer, and he is "tip-ping" God. Talking about twenty-five and thirty-five cents a week and he has the audacity to call it a tithe!" He could have tithed the milk he was feeding his cats and had more than that. Then one day it dawned on me that he wasn't to blame, I was. I was his pastor. I was trying to lead that church in an enlarging program, but up to that point, I had sold him on a thirty-five-cent program. I determined then never to propose a twenty-five-cent or thirty-five-cent program again. I determined to find someway of getting a program for a church that will challenge a man for the potential that God has placed in him and in his hands.

I believe that one of the tasks of stewardship of a church is from its own heart to develop and dedicate a program that is big enough to demand that a man examine his potential to see whether or not he is big enough for the program. Many people of great ability are not being used in our churches for the simple reason that we have never found any job big enough for them. They work five or six days as week in a job that is so much bigger than what the church asks them to do that they just don't have time for the church because they are too busy for the little things. Now it may not be right on their part to think these are little things for they are of eternal importance. But the fact is that we are not demanding the best of the man. I believe that the church needs to be a better steward of its manpower than that. We need to have plans big enough that the membership will have to examine themselves searchingly before the eyes of God to see whether or not they are big enough for the task, not whether that task is big enough to challenge them. The task should be so big that they would not dare attempt it without the power of God. The churches must be stewards of their manpower.

Lastly, a church must be a steward of its material resources. Many churches have been very poor stewards of their resources. Many churches have a poor complex. They think they are poor because they may see some other churches with bigger and better buildings. They may see some other churches with bigger budgets. They may see some other churches with more things to work with and they get the idea that "we are poor." The only thing that makes a church poor is when it thinks its poor. Because when all the wealth of God is available, it is a question of having faith enough to claim the promises of God. A church can do anything God expects it to do. If we will attempt to do what God expects us to do, it is God's business to provide the resources, not ours. Of course, we have to remember that when God provides the resources for a church, he doesn't put it in the offering plate. He puts it in the till. He doesn't put it in the treasury of the church, he puts it in the pockets of the members. So the members have to be faithful stewards for God to bless the church because that's the only way he does it. He doesn't rain pennies from heaven, he blesses businesses and farms and makes oil wells flow. That's the way God supports and blesses his churches. When the church has a program big enough to challenge its members, and a church has a program big enough to feel that it is doing what God wants it to do, then it has a perfect right to look up to God and say, "God, you move our hearts to lay down what is necessary." When it gets there, the church has to be faithful to do with it what God gave it to the church to do.

Some churches I have known through the years have not been too honest at this point. I found in a church one time that the money designated to go into missions had not been sent in four months. I asked the treasurer why. And he said, "Well, we just didn't have enough money to pay all the bills and pay missions, too." And I said, "Well, the treasurer's report that you have been bringing every month shows money going to missions." He said,

"It shows the amount of money that the budget said went to missions but I just didn't write the check." I don't know what you call that but it just isn't an honest financial report to me. I had to sit down with that man and a few other men and try to figure out a way to bring ourselves out of that mess. Here we had made a commitment of what we said we were going to do, and we didn't do it. I say that when we make a commitment of this sort, honesty demands that we do it. It's not the decision or the prerogative of the treasurer to decide which he is going to do. That's the business of the church.

I believe that when we look at ourselves as a church and when we look at our budget and we make commitments to missions; whether it is foreign missions, local missions, or home missions, this is God's program outside, the outreach, the long outreach, from our church. When we determine what God's will is for us to do in these matters and we set out to do it, we must either do it or back up and admit that we made a mistake. But if God called us to do it, then he intended us to do it. To say, "Well we spent too much over here," is not good stewardship. You see, a church can do the same thing that an individual can do. An individual can say: "I can't afford to tithe. I just had too many bills this month. I just don't have anything left over for my tithe." We say: "Well, he isn't a very good steward. His tithe ought to be his first tenth." Yet you can go to the business meetings of some churches and you will hear, "We couldn't send any money to missions this month because we had too many bills." Those churches weren't very good stewards. They should have found a way to have gotten by with less in order to give priority to that which goes to somebody else. That's a Christian priority and it is accomplished through honest stewardship.

Churches are stewards, too. I believe that churches need to commit themselves to these things, these principles and to live for them, to live on them and to live by them for the glory of God.

8.
Why I Tithe

In the summer of 1931 I was spending some of the summer vacation in my sister's home some six hundred miles from our home. During those few weeks, I came to that experience of accepting Jesus Christ as my personal Savior. Upon my return home, I of course, told my parents of my decision. My parents were Christians, my father was a preacher. They rejoiced in hearing of my decision to become a Christian. I remember something else that followed that announcement upon my return home.

My father took me aside to give me the instructions that he thought I needed. Among some other things he said: "Now son as a Christian there are some things that are expected of you, and you need to know about them so that you can do what you are expected to do. "First of all, since you have professed yourself to be a Christian, you're expected to publicly declare that faith and be baptized into some church in this community where you can grow up and serve your Lord." He said, "You know our family are all Baptists, but there are five churches in this town and it is your business as an individual to make a choice. If you're old enough to be a Christian, you're old enough to choose a church for yourself." So he said: "You find out what church you think is the closest to what you believe the New Testament to teach. If I can answer your questions, I will be glad to try, but the decision is yours." Well to make a long story short, I decided that if a Baptist church was good enough for my father, it was good enough for me, so I joined it, and I haven't regretted it. But the second thing he said to me I also have practiced and have not regretted it. He said: "Now, son when you have joined a church of your choice, Christians are expected to tithe and to support the church they belong to. I expect you to do the same, no matter which church you decide to join." Well, I didn't have the advantage of some of the boys and girls of that age today. I did not have a set allowance that came to me every week. I did not have any definite income that I could count on to say that this I could expect, except that I knew that from time to time my father would see to it that I had a little spending money. But since it was irregular and unpredictable, I took a little notebook and I kept a record of everything that I received so that I could honestly and faithfully see to it that when Sunday came, at least 10 percent of what I received was still with me. I knew that it had been the practice of my family, as well as my father, that we take at least 10 percent of all that we received with us to the church when we went to worship on Sunday. There in those small beginnings I learned to keep books, I learned to figure percentages, I learned to measure up to some responsibilities as a Christian and as a church member. It's over forty years since that habit began and I do not say it boastfully, but honestly that I do not remember missing a week in those years but what I have brought to the Lord the first tenth of what he has given to me.

There have been testimonies given from time to time from those who have begun tithing late in life and they talk about the increase in their income after they have started to tithe. I think I could outdo them on that score if I would compare my income in the summer of 1931 to what it is now. I'm not convinced, however, that it is totally due to the fact that I've been tithing all these years! There have been many other blessings, as well as material blessings, that have come into my life that I believe are directly attributable, not to my honesty with percentage points, but to the fact that I made a decision and a commitment to my God in which he and I have both had a part. There have been blessings for me and I hope glory for him.

The problem with us is that many times we fail to see the real point of all of this. To some people tithing is a scheme by which you raise money for churches. We learn from the book of Genesis that tithing is older than the Mosaic Law. I would not say that Abraham commenced it, though some would say so. But there is archaeological evidence that men of other religions in Abraham's time also gave 10 percent of their material wealth to the temple of their god. Then when Abraham did it, it was not any special revelation to him as an individual, but it was a special commitment by him as an individual in his relationship with his God no matter what other men of other religions did about it. It is said that in the New Hebrides there is a people, pagan in their religion, who eat pork and when they have finished eating the pig, they take the tail from the pig and go to the temple of their idol and they sacrifice it to their god. Dr. Ralph Grant, a pastor in Texas, says that far too many of us are "pig-tail living and giving" because we give only the leftovers to God.

Tithing is not just 10 percent. The whole spirit and principle to tithing goes far deeper than moving the decimal point one point over from your declared income. All through the Scriptures, it is declared to be the *first* tenth. It's not 10 percent of the take-home pay. That's where you get in trouble with the "ducks." It's when you let the "deducts" get into your religion; and you start looking at take-home pay after the deductions. The Lord said "the first tenth of all thine increase." Why sould I tithe?

It Is Scriptural

Someone asked a man some years ago if it didn't bother him that there were some verses of Scripture that he didn't understand. And he said, "No, it's the ones I understand that bother me." And I think that really is our problem in the stewardship of material things. It isn't that we don't understand it, it isn't that we can't figure it out, it is simply that we don't want to do it. What are some of the reasons, some of the motivations, for one accepting the biblical standard of tithing as evidence of his dedication to God? In the first place, it's scriptural.

We've already read the statement of Abraham, it was the declaration of his faith and the dedication of his life. Abraham practiced it. In the twenty-eighth chapter of Genesis, we find that his grandson, Jacob, practiced it as a matter of gratitude. You will remember that he had a dream. As he awakened in the morning he said, "Surely God was in this place and I knew it not." Then he rehearsed for himself the promise that God had given him in the dream. God would give success to the journey that he was on and to his life. He would provide for him materially and he would take him safely back to his home. And Jacob said: "If God will do these things for me, then the Lord shall be my God and I shall surely give him the tenth of all that he gives to me." As a matter of gratitude and of faith in God's promises, he declared the Lord to be his God and evidenced it by two things. He set there a pillar, he took the stone upon which he slept and set it up as a pillar for passersby to know that this is the place that Jacob met God and this is the place where Jacob dedicated himself to be a tither. Secondly, he made the commitment of his heart that all of that God gave him, he would give the tenth back to God. We read Leviticus 27 that Moses, as God's man giving the law to God's people, he included the law of the tithe. He did not initiate it, he did not begin it. It was not a new idea, but in here it became genuinely a part of worship and it became genuinely a part of God's revealed will for his people.

We go on to the book of Malachi, the third chapter, and we find as it were an echo from the words of Jacob. Jacob said, "The Lord is my God, therefore I will tithe." Moses said, "The tithe is the Lord's, it is holy unto him." Malchi said, "Ye have robbed God in that you have not brought the tithes and the offerings." They belong to God. Moses declared the tithe is the Lord's. If it is the Lord's, then it is not mine. That's like the Lord's Day, if it is the Lord's Day, then it is not mine. It's not for me to do what I please with the Lord's Day, because it is the Lord's and not mine. And the tithe, if it is the Lord's tithe, it is not for me to do with it what I wish, for it is not mine. It is only mine to bring. It's the Lord's tithe and it is holy and sacred, it is dedicated unto the Lord. Malachi the prophet declared that they were robbing God when they withheld the tithe.

Then we come to the New Testament and we find that Jesus taught it. He said to the Pharisees who were very scrupulous in the letter of the law, that they tithed and they ought to but they should not leave undone other things such as mercy and judgment and faith. You see tithing is no substitute. A man cannot be faced with the needs of mankind, material or spiritual, and say: "I have no personal responsibility to those things because I give my tithe Let the missionary go; let the preacher witness to the lost; let the benevolence committee take care of the human needs. I tithe, I fulfilled my duty." That's what the Pharisee said. And that's the reason he walked by on the other side of the street and let the Samaritan have the joy of administering to the beaten man. Jesus said: "You are leaving these other things undone and trying to cover it up by your money, but this won't work." "This ye ought to do," Jesus said, "but not to leave the other undone." Tithing is no substitute for personal service to the needs of men. But Jesus did commend the tithing. He said, "This ye ought to do," and if my Lord says I ought to do it, I believe I ought to do it.

In addition to this, I believe our Lord practiced it. Now you say, where's the verse for that? Well, this is one of those things that we say is an argument from silence. Jesus ate one day without washing his hands first. They criticized him for it. They saw him go into the house of a sinner to eat and they criticized him for it.

It came time to pay the taxes and they started a rumor around that Jesus wasn't going to pay his taxes. So he sent Peter down to catch a fish and by a miracle of a coin in the mouth of the fish, he and Peter both paid their taxes. Do you think that crowd would let him get by without bringing his tithe to the Temple without being criticized? If they criticize you for who you eat with, and if they criticize you for whether you wash your hands before you eat or not, and if they criticize you for not paying your taxes when they are not past due yet, you think they would not have criticized you for not tithing, if you failed to do it? Besides, do you think that our Lord would say to the Pharisees "ye ought to do it" and then not do it himself? Would you accuse our Lord of preaching and then not practicing? We are told in the Scriptures that Jesus habitually went to the place of worship on the day of worship and I believe he would have fulfilled the other command of the law when it says that they should not come into the house of the Lord empty-handed, but should always bring something to the Lord. I believe he would have brought at least the tithe.

In First Corinthians, chapter 16, the apostle Paul presents the principle of proportionate giving. He's talking about a special offering. In all probability these people had already been taught to tithe. They had not heard any preachers but Jewish preachers who had become Christians, and they would not have lessened the standards for the Christians from what they had been reared under as Jews. Jesus never lowered a single standard anywhere. You read the Sermon on the Mount as he took the law concerning morality and concerning material things, he never lowered a standard on anything for anybody. He raised it, but never lowered it. We find also in the teachings of our Lord that one third of his parables have to do with the proper use of material things, and one verse out of six in the Gospels have to do with man's proper use of material things. If it figured this large, this important, in the teachings of our Lord, then you and I ought not to take lightly our relationship and our responsibility with material things. In both the Old and the New Testaments, the principle and the spirit of tithing are included as the minimum of Christian responsibility.

It Is Spiritual

There is another reason. Not only is it scriptural but it is spiritual. Now this may come as a surprise to some people because tithing has seemingly been spelled with a dollar sign. They thought in terms of money. Well, it involves money. Christian dedication, Christian consecration always involves everything you possess or control as well as your self. This is merely the public declaration of it. Yes, the coin that you might hold in your hand, or the paper money that you might hold in your hand is material. You can see it, you can feel it, but tithing is an action, not a coin, not a currency. It's a spiritual action because it's for a spiritual purpose and with a spiritual motive. Is the money you possess moral or immoral? We find mention in the Scriptures, for example, of "filthy lucre." But what is it that makes lucre filthy? What is it that makes money dishonest? What is it that makes money tainted? It's not within the nature of the coin to be immoral. It's not within the nature of the currency to be immoral. Material things are always amoral. They are neither moral or immoral. And the thing that makes lucre filthy is the hand of the man that uses it. The thing that makes money immoral is the immorality of the man that spends it.

Had you ever thought about the so-called "blood money" that Judas threw on the floor of the Temple after he betrayed our Lord? Where did it come from? Had he not just a few hours before received it from the hands of a priest? And had not the priest received it as a tithe from a worshiper at the Temple? The same coin that was the sacred holy tithe of a faithful worshiper became the blood money of a Judas. The difference was not in the coin, the difference was in the man. If tithing is purely materialistic to you, it's not the fault of the coin, it's the fault of the man. It can gain spirituality by the way in which you use it. It can become moral. It can become humanitarian. It can become compassionate.

It can become worshipful. Yes, in the language of the Scriptures it can become holy when it is the dedicated portion of your material possessions, surrendered to God. It is spiritual.

Jesus said, "Lay not up treasures for yourself on earth, but lay up treasures in heaven." How can I do that? I can drive down the street and find the convenient drive-in windows where I can put money in the bank, but how can I put money in heaven? A wise man of our state of Texas some years ago studied that question and came to the decision, as his testimony was: "I've heard a lot of sermons on laying up treasures in heaven but no preacher ever told me how to get them there." He said, "I searched the Scriptures and I prayed to my God and I came to the conclusion that there was only one thing going to heaven and that was the souls of men. If my cattle and my ranches and my oil wells were going to be invested and deposited in heaven, then they are going to have to be spent on people." And when a Christian spends things on people because of Christian love and Christian devotion and Christian dedication, then his cattle and his ranches and his oil wells and his fruit orchards become spiritual.

Tithing is spiritual because of the purpose for which we bring it—to spread the gospel around the world and to minister to the spiritual needs and the spiritual growth and the maturity of the saved. And it is spiritual because of the dedication of my heart at the moment that I bring it to my God as an act of worship. This makes it spiritual. Jesus said, "Beware of covetousness," and then he told the story of the rich farmer, the selfish farmer, who had an abundant harvest. You see, God causes the rain to fall on the just and the unjust and sometimes the wicked and the selfish farmers will have as good a harvest as the Christian farmer. But here is the difference. Jesus said of the selfish farmer who could see nothing but the gathering of the grain unto himself, he was going to feast his soul on material wealth and he would build bigger barns in order to store it. He was busy trying to get it and to keep it. Jesus said of that man, "God shall say to him, this night thy soul shall be required of thee and then whose shall these things be? And so it is," Jesus said, "with every man who is not rich toward God, but layeth up treasures for himself." Yes, tithing is spiritual. It's one of the best preventives and cures for covetousness that I know of anywhere in the Bible. If it is done with the right spirit of dedication, so that my tithe becomes not something that would be a power and an influence in politics and business of my church, but comes as a public declaration of my dedication to God, then it is spiritual in its motive and its purpose and it is an investment in heaven and at the same time it will keep me from becoming selfish and covetous. Try it and see. If for no other reason than that, I would do it. I would practice it.

Some years ago I was advised by some in the medical fraternity that you can take medicine when you are sick but there are some kinds of medicine you can take before you get sick and if you take it at the right time and according to the right prescription you won't get sick, at least not with the disease that it is intended for. Some of you take flu shots. Some of you take one-a-day vitamins. Why? Because you want to prevent sickness. There is no sickness worse than the sickness of one's soul in covetousness and greed and the sinfulness of selfishness. It will shrivel your soul till you cannot see the greatness of our world, nor the glory of our God, nor will you ever be able to be sensitive to the feelings of mankind. Do you want to be that kind of coldhearted, feelingless being in a wonderful world like this? If you will first of all get your heart right with God through faith in Jesus Christ, getting right also in relationship to material things, then God will keep you from becoming a shriveled soul, a compassionless man, but rather will make you a concerned and compassionate Christian who becomes a co-laborer with God in his intention of redeeming the world from sin. It's scriptural and it is spiritual.

It Is Personal

Lastly, it is personal. My reasons for tithing are very personal.

Some people say that it is so personal that it's private. "I don't want anybody to know about it." They misquote that verse from Jesus, "Let not your left hand knoweth what your right hand doeth." Jesus was talking about the way in which you help the poor man on the street. When you get ready to drop that noisy little dime into the blind man's tin cup, you look around to see who's going to watch you. You need not bother, they will hear you! Just go ahead and drop it. But don't treat God like he was a blind man with a tin cup. You see we don't tip God like we do a waitress. Tithing is an entirely different thing.

I don't want to be small with God. I want to do what God expects me to do. And he blesses us accordingly. Yes, it is personal, but it is not private. I'm willing to do it openly. I have never in twenty-five years of the ministry performed a baptismal service privately, it's always performed publicly with everybody free to come and see. And I'm not ashamed of being a tither either. Because I feel it is the only honest thing to do. I don't go around privately and secretly paying my bills so that no one will know about it. If I am ashamed of the bill, I ought not to have made the purchase. If I am ashamed of my relationship with God, I ought not to have made the covenant. But being not ashamed of it, I openly declare myself, and my relationship with my Lord.

There are some other reasons. I want that preventative blessing that comes, keeping me from being covetous, but I also want that sense in my own mind and heart that I'm having a part in what God wants done in this world. He gave his Son on Calvary's cross. Jesus died for our sins and rose from the dead and then one day he gave a commission to his disciples to proclaim the good news to all the world. From that day to this, this has been done most effectively through his churches and if I want to have a part in what Jesus died for, I'm going to have to do it through the church where my membership is. So I do not only put my time and my talents, but I also place my tithe at the disposal of my church, for that way I feel that I am doing something of what Jesus would do.

Lastly, one day I am going to stand before my Lord and there's going to be a stewardship accounting. The scriptures say that "everyone of us shall give an account of himself to God." It's a stewardship report. The stewardship of time, what I have done with my years whether it is three score and ten, or just three score, or just the ten. Everyone of us shall give an account of his years to God. There is also going to be an accounting for our talents, what we have done with the abilities that God has given us. But in addition to this, we will given an accounting for all the things that we have used. One-third of the parables of Jesus, remember, had to do with the accounting of our stewardship of material things. Perhaps the other two-thirds had to do with talents and time. One verse out of six in the gospels indicates that you and I shall give an accounting to God.

9.
Tithing Is God's Plan

One of the failures, one of the sins, of the human race has always been the natural tendency to try to match wits with God and try to figure out substitutes that are just as good as what God said. Men have been doing this all through human history. We can go clear back to the Garden of Eden and find the record of one of the boys of Adam who made the same mistake. He thought he had a plan that was just as good as God's, but it wasn't and it was not acceptable to God. Men have been doing the same thing in our own generation. We, too, have made substitutions. Some people have substituted an organization of one sort or another in the community as a substitute for the church and have thought that because they were busy at good deeds they were serving God. Some have thought that so long as they didn't substitute something for water, the method in which it was used would be just as good, so long as you called it baptism. And so we have come along to the plan of maintaining the work of God and we have come up with substitutes.

I pastored in a rural community early in my ministry and everybody in the community but the Baptists were promoting what they called "God's Acre Plan." They took one acre out of their field each year and took the harvest from that one acre and brought it to their church house and they had an auction and sold it and gave that money to the church. That was the way some of the churches in that community were supported. Sounds good, but it's a substitue. It's not God's plan. I can go back a little farther in my memory and remember that I grew up in a church that had another plan. I lived in the county seat and so the county fairgrounds was at our town. I can remember when the women of the Baptist church in our town sold hamburgers in a stand out at the county fair every year. I can also remember when the women had more money in their treasury than the church had. In fact, I remember when the church voted to borrow some money from the Ladies' Aid to pay the pastor's salary. That's the kind of thing that can heppen when you use a substitute.

You see, God does have a plan, but we get mixed up sometimes in our vision and our concepts and some people talk about "paying the preacher." I can remember when that's the way it was because all the program they had was the preacher. And if he didn't come that Sunday, nothing happened. But there are churches that have more than a preacher. There are churches that are ministering by the life of the congregation, by the work of the people ministering in the name of the Lord, and that's a program, not just a preacher. But some people still think of it in terms of paying the preacher.

Some people think of supporting the church, and when they think of supporting the church, they think in terms of maintaining the building and trying to keep the front steps from falling down and keeping the lights turned on and that sort of thing. They think this is providing for the church because they've lost their vision. They've failed to remember that the church is not a building. It's the people of God who are supposed to be doing the work of God, and so I believe that the best way of thinking of God's plan in these matters is to think in terms of supporting the *work* of the Lord. Supporting the work of the Lord: the preacher might be a part of that; the church building might be a part of that but there are a thousand other things just as important, perhaps more important. It's the work of the Lord to bring his redemptive message to the hearts and the minds of people around the world. What is God's plan for supporting his work? He has a plan. Has he revealed it to us or have we been left to our own wisdom and our own design to sit down somehow in a council meeting and discuss it, and discuss the needs and try to ascertain the requirements and the responsibilities and then by some business acumen come up with a solution that will raise the amount of money that's needed? God's plan is not a fund-raising campaign. God is concerned about two things, really. In the first place, he is concerned about his own people, like a father is concerned about the rearing of his boys— teaching them, training them, disciplining them, making men of them. God is concerned about this. God is also concerned about the proclamation of his message of love and grace and truth to all men, everywhere. God's basic concern is people, people.

We do God an injustice when we accept the attitude that God is concerned about money. God is concerned about money like he is concerned about buildings. God is concerned about money and buildings like you and I might be concerned about an automobile. It's a means to an end. But God's end, God's purpose, God's objective is people. Let us never lose sight of this. God is concerned about the disciplining, the teaching, the training of his own people, like a father his family, but he is also concerned about the ultimate purpose of his family—that that family might be enlarged by the redemption, by the regeneration of multitudes of others. This cannot happen until they hear the gospel of Jesus Christ. What is God's plan that can accomplish both of these at the same time? It's really quite simple. It's not new.

Divine in Origin

We can go back to the book of Genesis and find it. As we read it in the fourteenth chapter, we find it very expressly stated there. This is the first mention of the word "tithe." However, we know from other sources than the Bible that tithing was not limited to the Hebrews. It was practiced by the Babylonians and many others who did not worship Jehovah at all. But somehow it was a gener-ally accepted concept that one tenth of the harvest was to be brought into the house of their god, whatever their god might be. We find that so far as our Christian heritage is concerned and so far as the biblical revelation is concerned that it began with Abraham.

Abraham was coming back from Babylon where he had done battle to preserve the life of his nephew, Lot. He made an interest-ing statement that has come true in many instances even in our own day. He stood there before Melchizedek. And the Bible says that Abraham "presented to him tithes of all." That is, of the spoils of the battle. He was giving tithes. They had taken captives to be slaves. They had taken spoils of material possessions, and there they were bringing it all back with them from their conquered people. And the priest said, "just give me the slaves, the prisoners, just give me the people, but you take the things, the goods." And Abraham said, "No, you're going to take the tithes of the whole thing. Don't tell me to tithe part of it. I'm going to tithe it all. "If I held back any of it you would say that you made Abraham rich." Abraham wasn't going to get rich off the withheld tithe! He was going to be honest with his tithe, so that if he became rich it would be by the blessing of God and not by the dishonesty or the failure to be faithful to God in the realm of his stewardship of material things. Abraham said, "I'm not going to have the priest telling me that he made me rich because he gave me the tithe that I should have given to him."

In the twenty-eighth chapter of Genesis we find the grandson of Abraham. You remember that the grandson of Abraham left home because of the difficulty he was having with his brother and he was headed toward his mother's people. He had a vision, a vision in which he saw the angels ascending and descending from heaven on a ladder. We are all familiar with that story of Jacob's ladder, or Jacob's dream, but many times we forget what happened after he awakened in the morning. He realized that God was in this place. So this place where he had had a holy experience with God, he named Bethel, the place of God, the house of God. And then it says that Jacob vowed a vow, that he said, "If God will be with me and will keep me in this way that I go and will give me bread to eat and raiment to put on, so that I come again to my Father's house in peace, then shall the Lord be my God." Here was a testimony of personal faith. The Lord, the Lord of Abraham and Isaac was about to become the Lord of Jacob. Jacob was willing to acknowledge him as the God, the Lord of his life, the object of his worship, on the basis that he had learned that God was the one that provides for his life. He said, this being true, he'll be my Lord and this stone which I have set for a pillar shall be God's house. I like to think of that pillar that he set there for any wayfarer, any stranger passing by to see, like a monument. There he had made a sign of a pledge. He had made a covenant with God and left a monument to testify of it. It wasn't any secret that he was trying to keep to himself, but he erected a monument in the place to remember the day in which he entered into covenant with Almighty God. And he said, "This shall be God's house and of all that thou shalt give me I will surely give the tenth unto thee."

When I was in college, my Bible professor, Dr. Lawrence W. Cleland, said one day, "The best way to make a tither is to convert his grandfather." Well, that's what happened here. Abraham was a tither. Nothing is said about Issac one way or the other, but his grandson came up with it. I don't think that it was any isolated idea that cropped up in his mind. I think this was the culmination of a committment that had been taught him from his grandfather and his father.

I remember the time when I became a Christian. When I came home and told my father that I had accepted Christ as my Savior, he said, "Son, there are some things that you need to know." He said, we're happy about your decision, but there are some other things you need to know, and so he explained some things to me. And then he explained to me about tithing. My father was a tither.

My grandfather was a tither. And my father explained to me from the Scriptures what was expected of me. I remember that I kept a record of the nickels and dimes that I was given here and there, and earned by extra jobs and one thing and another, so when Sunday came I would know what I had received that week and be ready to take to church with me a tithe of all that I had received. This was the way my father brought me up. And when I read that Jacob, out in a lonely place, after a night's experience with Almighty God came up with a covenant like this, I don't believe that Jacob thought it up for himself. I think his father Isaac had told him this would be expected of him. I think his grandfather's example had been carried on as a tradition and a heritage of that family, and it's a glorious thing when a family learns to tithe.

We can go on down through the Scripture record and we find that Moses, the great man of God who was given the laws of God in Mt. Sinai, explained them to the whole people of Israel. Generations had gone by in which they had failed to worship as they ought to have worshiped many times. In Egypt in bondage, they didn't have religious freedom. And they many times failed to do what God would have had them do if they had been a free people in a free land. God had to give them written instructions, and with his own finger, the Scripture says, he wrote it in tablets of stone and gave it to Moses, and he brought it down from the mountain and explained it to the people. One of the things that he explained was something that Abraham and Isaac and Jacob had practiced. Some people say, "Well, tithing, that's law and we're under grace." Tithing is not a matter of law. Tithing was practiced by God's people four hundred years *before* the law was given to Moses. The law simply recorded it for a new generation that which needed to be taught. Tithing is God's plan for supporting God's work. So he revealed it to Moses and through Moses to the people. "All the tithe of the land, whether the seed of the land, or the fruit of the tree is the Lord's: it is holy unto the Lord" (Lev. 27:30).

We find also that Solomon, the man known for his wisdom,

recorded in the third chapter of the book of Proverbs that there was a vital relationship between a man and his God and material things. Solomon doesn't use the word tithe, but those things that Abraham and Jacob said of it are certainly indicated in what Solomon said about it when he says: "Honor the Lord with thy substance, and with the firstfruits of all thine increase: so shall thy barns be filled with plenty, and thy presses shall burst out with new wine" (Prov. 3:9–10). When a man becomes a co-partner with God, the God that provides the fertility of the soil and the fertility of the seed, the God that provides the sun and the rain, can do some mighty marvelous things. When man, the only one of God's creation that has a free will, will freely choose to cooperate with God, some marvelous things can happen. And Solomon mentioned some of them in material terms, because that's what he was talking about.

Over in the book of Nehemiah we find another man, the prophet Nehemiah who came to help rebuild Jerusalem and the house of God and the land of God. He came back, after he had been away. Time had elapsed, and he found that the house of God was empty. He found that the Levites who were supposed to have been singing in the choir weren't there. He said, "The singers are out in the fields." Now that may not mean much to you unless you stop and reflect on the fact that when God had laid out through Joshua the division of the Promised Land, the Levites, the tribe of Levi, were not given any land. Levi and his descendants were to be the servants of God in the house of God and the other tribes were to bring the tithes of the land to the house of God and "the tithe of the tithe was the inheritance of the Levites." They should not be busy in the fields, they should be busy in the house of God, taking care of God's work as it pertained to the house of the Lord. Nehemiah found they weren't there. They weren't doing the work of the Lord. The house of God was neglected and it was empty. He searched around and found that the day of God was being neglected. They were violating the sabbath. I don't know whether they were going fishing or hunting or boating or what they were doing. They might have been just sitting on their back porch, but they were not worshiping God on the Lord's Day. And Nehemiah found also that they were violating the marriage laws and they were intermarrying with pagans. The marriage laws, the sabbath law, and the law of material stewardship were all being violated. The house of God was rundown and neglected. The treasuries were empty and the servants of God were out working in the fields where they were forbidden to be by God.

"So Nehemiah said: "I perceived that the portions of the Levites have not been given them: for the Levites and the singers, that did the work, were fled every one to his field. Then contended I with the rulers and said, Why is the house of God forsaken? And I gathered them together and set them in their place. Then brought all Judah the tithe of the corn and the new wine and the oil unto the treasuries. And I made treasurers over the treasuries" (Neh. 13:10–13). We decry the spiritual conditions of America today. It is my personal conviction that America will not have a spiritual revival that will change the moral conditions of this nation until the churches of America have a stewardship revival that will make the people of God honest with God as Nehemiah had to do with them in Judah. That's the word of God, that's the plan of God. Until you get a man right in his relationship between things and God, he is not going to be right between himself and his neighbor. As long as a man will rob God he will rob his neighbor, if he has to knock him in the head on the street after dark to do it. Immorality, the neglect of the house of God, the desecration of the day of God, all of these things are the outgrowth of a man's failure to be right with God in his own heart.

Malachi, another prophet, looked at the conditions of his nation in his day and he described the drought that could come and some of the pestilences that could come and some of the sorrows that could come and bring a nation into poverty. And he gave them the explanation, if you will bring the tithe that belongs to the Lord into the house of the Lord, then the Lord will provide for you. "That there might be meat in my house." Malachi said.

In the New Testament you will find that Jesus talked about tithing. In the twenty-third chapter of Matthew, and also in the eleventh chapter of Luke it's recorded that he had some things to say about tithing. He looked at those Pharisees, religious people, morally righteous people, meticulous about their religious doings, but they were wrong in their relationship to people. Jesus said to them, "Woe unto you scribes and Pharisees, hypocrites, for ye pay tithe" (notice he was talking to tithers now, not nontithers). He said, "Ye pay tithes of the mint, the anise, and the cummin," that's the little things of the garden even, "but you have omitted the weightier matters of the law, judgment, mercy, and faith. These ought ye to have done and not to leave the other undone." Jesus said, "ye ought to do."

You can find tithing mentioned again in the seventh chapter of Hebrews, where the writer of Hebrews is comparing Melchizedek and Christ and uses the fact that Abraham paid tithes to Melchizedek and we pay tithes to Christ. There is more to it than this, even.

It Is Definite in Method

The Scripture says that all things should be done decently and in order. I believe that as we worship our God, whether it's in the singing of our songs or whether it's the preaching of our sermons or the offering of our prayers or the bringing of our tithes and offerings, I believe we ought to be definite in our commitment. The Scriptures tell us that there must be a definiteness, or if there's an uncertain sound to the trumpet, who's going to go to war? There needs to be a definiteness, and I believe that God has given us a definite plan. It's not something that's left open to play with. It's not an optional thing, except as you and I always have the option of obeying, or disobeying God. We have the option of whether we want to be saved or not, if you want to call that an option. We have an option of choosing to serve God and to obey God, or take the consequences of not doing so. But God has given to us a definite plan.

It's so definite that it stands out in bold relief when Paul was writing to the Christians in Corinth about a special offering of benevolence. He didn't use the word tithe and I really don't think he was talking about tithing. I think he was talking about an offering over and above the tithe. In the background are the basic principles of Christian stewardship, when he says, "every one of you." (that's a definite person) "on the first day of the week," (that's a definite time); "lay aside as God has prospered you," (that's a definite proportion); and for a definite purpose, he said, "so there won't be any collections when I come."

Paul said, "I don't want any collections when I come." He was not in the fund-raising business. He was in the business of preaching the gospel. He said, "when I go to Jerusalem I'll carry your offering with me," but he wasn't going to be involved in raising money. He was busy raising the children of God. There is something definite. It calls for a definite commitment. A lady said to me some years ago: "We've never figured the tithe, but we figure we give more than the tithe." And I said: "Lady, if you don't figure the tithe, I don't figure you tithe." If you are not willing to face up to facts and figures in simple percentages that any schoolboy can figure out, you're trying to evade the real issue. You're not definite in your commitment. You're just giving as it strikes you, as you feel like, on Sunday.

What's the basis of your giving? Is it a definite commitment to God? I feel that as I said from the experience of my father's instruction shortly after my conversion to Jesus Christ, that from that day to this I have never failed to tithe because somehow my commitment to the Lord publicly in baptism and in church membership and my commitment to the Lord in the stewardship of material things as expressed in tithing were a part of my commitment to Christ as the Lord of my life and I date it back to the time of my conversion. When I became a Christian I had the desire to go all the way and my father told me what that meant and as best as I've known how, I've done it from that day until this. I knew a man some years ago was not a Christian. He later became one, but for years before he was a professing Christian he tithed. He said, "I know that all I have belongs to God whether I've given him my heart yet or not." At least he could read. He could read the Word of God.

It Is Dignified in Practice

It's not only a definite thing, it's the decent thing. Paul said to Timothy, "a man that does not provide for his own, especially those of his own house, denies the faith and is worse than in infidel" (See 1 Tim. 5:8). We've thought about this, a Christian man as the head of the house, providing for his family. He has a responsibility and it's a part of his Christian witness to provide for his family. I believe the same kind of commitment, the same kind of standard stands there before you and me today, not only for the sake of our families, but for the sake of our church. For a man that does not support his own, his own home, his own church, denies the faith. He professes to be a member of it. He professes to be a part of it, and yet in the very necessities of its working and its ongoing, he'll take no part of it. He denies his commitment. He denies his faith because he does not support the work of God through the church in which he claims to be a part. This is part of the commitment we make to the Lord Jesus Christ. We're not only stewards of our bodies and stewards of our minds and stewards of our lives, but we're stewards of our possessions.

10.
If I Die Before I Wake

Luke 12:13-31

It has been said that no man is prepared to live until he is prepared to die. Many of us assume that we will live until a ripe old age—or at least until tomorrow. That is the reason we leave for tomorrow some things that we ought to do today. Luke 12: 13–31 tells of a man who could not cope with success! This story raises some valid questions for our consideration.

Whose Shall These Things Be?

Several years ago when I was pastoring a church that was in a program of selling bonds to build a mission building, I visited a certain funeral director in that community to sell him some bonds. He said, "What makes you think I've got any money?" I said, "Well, my Bible says that they didn't take it with them, and I figured that this was the last place they could leave it." Well, he bought some bonds. Have you stopped to realize that you can't take it with you? The Scripture declares very plainly, "We brought nothing into this world, and it is sure we will carry nothing out." That's one of the laws of life. It's built into it, some that what things come to our hands during these years are things that we can use while we're here. But then we're confronted with the question that God confronted the rich man with, "Then whose shall they be?"

A widow tells the story of the experience that was hers at the time of her husband's death. They didn't have a joint bank account. All of the family's funds were frozen. The lock box containing their insurance papers and other things were sealed by the Internal Revenue Department. Until the court was able to meet, she didn't have funds for funeral expenses. She did not have funds for living expenses. She didn't have funds, period. She was named by the court as the guardian of her child, and she was named by the court as the executrix of the estate but had to be under bond in order to perform. That cost money. There were attorney fees and court fees, and she had to have a complete financial report to the penny of the expenditure of all funds and have her report notarized in turning it in to the court regularly until her son became of age, when what funds there were could be divided, his portion and her portion as the law prescribed. All of this because her husband came to the same day and the same hour that this farmer came to without being able to honestly answer the question "and then whose shall these things be?" because he died without making a will. I suppose he felt that there just isn't much to leave. But he left a son that was a ward of the court, not because he was without a mother, but because his father died without a will. That's the law. God was not being a harsh judge. He was asking a very simple, straight-forward, everyday question, "If you die before you wake, then whose shall these things be?"

Now that points out the fact that we are accountable to God. It was God that asked the question. This puts this whole story into perspective then, into perspective with the story in Genesis when God made Adam and put him in the garden and told him to take care of it for him. Man was never intended to be anything but a gardener. It was never intended that man should claim and possess things for himself. We find the New Testament Christians shortly after an experience with the Holy Spirit that gave them an insight and a vision into the meaning of life they'd never had before: "And none of them said that ought of the things he possessed was his own." We recognize that man is a trustee. He is the manager of something that does not belong to him.

We commonly use the word "stewardship." "Trusteeship" is just as good a word and maybe it will help to overcome some of our blind spots. Some of us just go blind with the glitter of gold when somebody says "stewardship." Stewardship, basically, is not really a matter of money at all. Stewardship, trusteeship, is a matter of relationship to God. That tells me what I am. That tells me how I am supposed to relate to God in this world. You see, there's more to life than things. But first we have to understand who I am and how I relate to God. And it's declared in the fourteenth chapter of Romans, "Every one of us shall give an account of himself to *God*" (14:12). Perhaps we could quote that again a little differently. "Every one of us shall give an account of *himself* to God." Just as this man had to given an account to God—an account of *himself,* an accounting of his possessions, not only for his span of years here, but what was to be done with it if he were to die before he wakes. All that comes into our hands is our responsibility, not just 10 percent. Some people think that they have fulfilled their trusteeship by being a tither. That's only the beginning. But all of the things that have come into a man's control or a woman's control, all of it, how it is spent or saved, how it is used or misused during our years, and how it is disposed of when our years on earth have come to close; we have a responsibility for the total.

I suppose if we knew exactly what day and what hour we were going to die, we would find some way of getting it all spent first. Then we wouldn't have any problem about whose it's going to be. We would already have it spent. And it looks some days like some young people are determined to do that—spend it all before life is over. But then as we grow a little older we become a little concerned that we might have it all spent before life is over. That problem we've had all along of having part of the month left over when the money is gone, can be magnified and enlarged by having some years left over when the money is gone. Then we spend our latter years in poverty when, if we have been a little wiser, we could have provided for them. Somewhere in here there is that haunting question of how we will use it and how we will save it and how we will leave it. There's one sure thing about it. You'll leave it!

The old question, "How much did he leave?" is promptly and rightly answered, "every bit of it." For you can take none of it with you. We are not going to leave it as if we just got up and walked off. But the day, the hour, and the moment, the second will come when we'll be taken from it. And if I die before I wake, whose shall these things be? God asked the question; we'll have to answer it.

How Shall I Account for My Life?

There's a second question here. And that's the question that I have already eluded to, "How shall I account for my life?" Underlying the first question is a more basic question of the man himself. For the stature of a man, the reputation of the man, the wealth of the man at the time of his death is really the lengthening shadow of his life. How shall I account for my life? That's more than accounting for the money. Money is coined personality. Time, the stuff of which life is made, goes into the making of money. Energy and strength, which is also a part of which life is made, goes into the making of money and the Scripture says that the strength to gain wealth is a gift from God (See Deut. 8:18.)

There's no indication that there is any sin in making money. You can make it sinfully, but just the matter of making money is not sinful. God didn't criticize this farmer for being a successful farmer. He did not criticize him for the abundant harvest. He only criticized him for the way he was expecting to use it, which really was a reflection or a shadow of the way he'd lived. When it came to thinking of how he could dispose of his success, he thought only in terms of keeping it and really not disposing of it at all. How can I store it? This was the story of his life. How can I keep it? That's a life to be accounted for.

The life includes more than things. Jesus said, "A man's life consisteth not in the abundance of the things which he possesseth."

Well, now then, of what does it consist? For the sake of simplicity and perhaps oversimplification let me say that life consists of purpose, passion, and power. Life is not intended to be meaningless. To live without meaning is not to live at all. Life calls for a purpose. We need to say this not only to our toddlers and our teen-agers, we need also to say it to those who are tottering. Life is to have purpose, and the purpose of a man's life dare not be bound up totally in things, for that's to live for material things alone and that's not to really live at all. Life has purpose, but it must have a spiritual purpose. It must be a purpose that's worthy of a creature that is created in the image of the Almighty God.

Life must also consist of passion. This involves the things to be loved and the things to be hated. This involves the things that would call upon our hearts for feeling in life. For a man to try to go through life without passion is to go through life cold and not to find any of the warmth of friendship in life at all. And that's a lonely way to live. Life is intended to have friends. Life is intended to have passion in it. There are some things we're supposed to hate. There are some things we are supposed to love. There are some things we're supposed to live for. There are some things we're supposed to die for. Life needs to have a passion in it. We need to live with a passion in relationship to other people—that means living with compassion.

But there also needs to be power in life. Life in its meaning, in its consistency calls for power, not power to rule as a tyrant in the world, but every man has his influence. It may be the influence of his smile. It may be the influence of his mind. It may be the influence of his highly trained and disciplined life. It may be the influence of his working hours. It may be the influence of his leisure hours. It may be the influence of his personality. It may be the influence of his money. The influence of his house as it stands in its place and in relationship to the houses and homes around it. It may be the influence of his business ventures, his farming or whatever it might be as it has an effect and a testimony on those who know of it. Influence. Power is not only the power of a ruler. Power is the influence of a life to affect other lives for good or evil. Christians have power, not necessarily the power of a throne though there have been and are Christian monarchs. It's not always the power of a political office though there have been and are Christian people in such places. But the power of God in one's life by which his life and all that it consists of can influence other people toward that which has become the center of his own life, even God. We're going to give an account of our lives to God. "Everyone of us shall give an account of himself," not just his money, but himself. His very soul, the way it's loved and the way it's lived shall be a part of his trustee report, part of his stewardship report. For everyone of us, the Scripture says "shall stand before the judgment bar of God. Every one of us shall give an account of himself to God."

The famous singer, Harry Lauder, said that in his childhood the lamplighter of his little town always started his evening rounds at the Lauder home and then zigzagged down the street lighting the lamps. He said that as a boy he often watched the lamplighter going about his work in the evening. He said as the lamplighter walked on down the street lighting the lamps, it would not be long until he was out of sight. But he said, "I could always tell where the lamplighter was because I could see the lights from where he'd been." There will come the evening of life when you and I shall walk beyond the sight of those with whom we've lived and loved, but they'll know where we've been and where we are by the lights we've left behind. We'll give an account of our lives to God.

Benjamin Franklin, the famous American, left a gift when he died. He determined who should have it when he died. As a result of that gift, a library was built in Philadelphia. Another man, an unknown man, left a comparable amount of money buried. Some men doing some excavation in Philadelphia found the money, but it had been buried so long that the paper money was so corrupted that it was useless. The men took the coins and went around the corner to the saloon and bought a few beers. One man was unknown. The other man will never be forgotten. All of it on the basis of the life that they had lived and how they determined what should be done with what they had after they had gone.

If I die before I wake, will anybody know I have been here? Will they know it by the lights I have left burning behind in somebody else's life? Will they know it by something I have left materially that will go on being used as a blessing because I so determined it before I died? Or willl they simple find the corrupted ashes of a life that's been lived and lost? "For what profiteth a man if he gain the whole world and lose his own soul?" If I die before I wake. . . . Do you have purpose in your life? Do you have a passion for living? Do you have a power that you are using for the glory of God?

We're going to give an account of this life. We ought to plan it. We may not live long enough to carry out our plans, but that's God's business. A life that is not planned is a life that for all practical purposes may not really be lived at all because we are living beneath our potential and living far short of our purpose, that is, the purpose of our Creator in creating us. If I die before I wake, I want to be able to give an accounting to God for the years I've had whether there be just this many as I've had until now, or whether I have another twenty or thirty or forty. I want to be lived up to the present opportunities and not have to face my God with regrets of what I didn't do simply because I didn't plan to do them, or simply because I planned to but I put them all off into the future by procrastination. I wasted a life. If I die before I wake, I want to be able to give a report that will be satisfactory to the Lord.

What About My Soul?

But there is a third question that comes out of this. God said unto him, "Thou fool, this night thy soul shall be required of thee." Not only was there a requirement of accounting for his life as it had been lived, not only was there an accounting for the material things that would be left as the residue of his life, but there was a deeper question than this and that is the simple question of our souls themselves, that spiritual essence of life, what of it? If I die before I wake, there will my soul go? This man was a fool, Jesus said. The word that's translated "fool" here is an interesting word. It doesn't necessarily mean that he was stupid, incapable of making plans or incapable of anticipating the values of life. But it is a word that literally translated means "without sense." That is, a man who is not necessarily without possession of sense, but who isn't using sense. Sometimes we admonish our children and our young people and others, "Don't be foolish," or "don't be so senseless." We're not saying that they're devoid of intellect. We're saying they're not using what God gave them. That's the kind of fool this man was. He had sense enough to plant a field, he had sense enought to look at a harvest and know that it was larger than his barns and his graineries. But he didn't use that same sense to know that there would come an hour when these things would do him no good. He said, as a soliloquy: "I will say to my soul, Soul, thou hast much goods laid up for many years, take thine ease, eat, drink, and be merry." There are two things wrong with that statement, at least.

In the first place, he was saying that his soul, that spiritual essence of life and self, could feast upon the harvest of the field. The Word of God says: "Man shall not live by bread alone, but by every word that proceedeth out of the mouth of God." There is a part of man that has to be fed by God on heavenly manna, the bread of life, and it doesn't come from the fields of earth. Someone has said, "A man's soul cannot eat things but the things of the world can eat at a man's soul." Dr. Herschel H. Hobbs, in interpretating this verse, says that the literal translation is, "This night these things are requiring thy soul of thee," noting that here was a man's life that was being consumed by things. That's what it was living for. And while he was doing it, he was dying in it because the real meaning of life was being increasingly lost by his increasing involvement and passion for things always wanting to keep it instead of giving it.

The second error he made in that short soliloquy was, "thou hast much goods laid up for *many years.*" He failed to use his intellect to observe that life is not guaranteed. He failed to recognize that no man as a ninety-nine year lease on life. He said, "Many years" but God said, "This night." What then? We can lay up our store and we can lay out our plans for what we will do if we live, but we must in all honesty underscore the word "if." Because while you and I are talking about tomorrow, and tomorrow, and tomorrow, God may say tonight! And if I die before I wake, where will my soul go?

In the book of Galatians, the apostle Paul tells us that a man must determine this by where he invests his life. For he says: "Be no deceived; God is not mocked: for whatsoever a man soweth, that shall he also reap. For he that soweth to his flesh, shall of the flesh reap corruption." (That's like the coins and paper corrupted because they were buried in the earth.) "But he that soweth to the Spirit shall of the Spirit reap life everlasting." (Gal. 6:7–8)

Would you today prepare to live by preparing to die?

11.
Stewardship at Home
Luke 12:13-21; 1 Timothy 5:1-8

Jesus said, "To whomsoever much is given, much shall be required." Just as a man who has an income of $20,000 a year has more to account for than a man who has $5,000, so parents of five children have more to account for than parents of one child. Accountability is really what stewardship is all about. Families are gifts from God, and we are just as accountable for these gifts as we are other gifts.

God has always worked through families. He called Abraham and started a new family. When that family became a nation with a throne and a king, he still referred to them as "the children of Israel." When God tried to reveal through Jesus what it was like to be related to God and to anticipate heaven, he talked in family terms. Jesus taught his disciples to pray "Our Father who art in heaven." The family and home are a biblical concept that has come to us from God himself.

Children—a Gift from God

The home and the family are a gift from God. God said to Joshua, "I led your father, Abraham, from beyond the floods and on through the lands of Canaan and I multiplied his seed and I gave him Isaac." Jacob said to Esau, "These are the children that God has graciously given to me." When Joseph introduced his children to their grandfather, Jacob, he said, "These are the sons that God has given me."

The biblical concept is that even children are a gift from God. As parents we face the question about whether or not we have really given the facts of life to our children, not just the biological facts of life but the facts concerning the truth that they are a gift from God. Do we realize and do we let our children know that each of us is somehow a special creation of God? And because our children, our families, are a gift from God, we are accountable to God for what we do with them.

Parents Are Responsible

As parents, we are accountable for all that goes into the making of family life. In the twelfth chapter of Luke, Jesus talked to the disciples about some of the accountability relationships in life. He spoke about a steward. The word "steward" as we find it used in the New Testament is one that means a "house manager." Stewardship at home. This is the word from which we get our word "economics," also. It has to do with the economics of the home. But when you come to manage a house, there are a lot of responsibilities besides managing money.

If family living is to be successful, is a home is to be effective to the purpose for which God established the concept of home and family, there must be management in it. There must be some setting of priorities, making of plans, and carrying out of purposes. This kind of home management is a responsibility of parents.

Parents are responsible first of all to determine the priorities in the home. Paul said, in writing to the Ephesians, "Bring up your children in the nurture and admonition of the Lord and provoke them to wrath." This is a parental responsibility. Children may not be in position on the basis of experience and knowledge to make a choice. Parents must set the priorities.

Along with those priorities, there must also be some plans. Jesus spoke of principle, not just a story, when he talked about the need to make a decision and the need to count the costs in becoming a Christian in the first place. It is a principle that is applicable in the building of a home and a family. If we are going to provide for our families as we ought to, it takes some planning. Planning involves thinking about money, but it involves more than that. What have we planned to give of ourselves for our family. Are our families really a part of the plan of our lives? If not, then we have not really planned.

Parental responsibility calls for provision, actual material provision. It is a responsibility of a Christian to provide for his family—provide for them in accordance with the priorities that have been established, provide for them in accordance with the plans that have been made. This is a part of our Christian faith; it is a part of home management; it is what the Bible is talking about in terms of stewardship.

The Image of God

Parents are responsible in the sight of God to maintain before the children an image. Man is created in the image of God. God used the language of parents to describe his relationship to people. Stewardship of a parental image—by the way we live, the way we speak, the priorities of our lives, the way we spend our money, we say to our children what God is like.

This is what stewardship of home is all about. Is your home so dedicated to the lordship of Christ that it serves his purpose?